Our Lady of Sorrows

Our Lady of Sorrows

A Compilation of the Teachings
of St. Alphonsus Liguori

Edited
by
Charles D. Fraune

2025
Slaying Dragons Press Classics

Our Lady of Sorrows is comprised of various sections within *The Glories of Mary*, the 1888 edition first published by P.J. Kennedy & Sons. These reprinted sections were carefully reviewed and occasional errors in the original have been corrected.

The Foreword includes an introduction taken from the Preface to the first volume of the Ascetical Works, from the Centenary Edition, edited by Rev. Eugene Grimm, Priest of the Congregation of the Most Holy Redeemer, originally published in 1887.

Cover design by Caroline Green. Image: *Mater Dolorosa*, by Carlo Dolci, 1655.

www.SlayingDragonsPress.com
2025

DEDICATION

To Our Lady of Sorrows,
Our most powerful Advocate

"From the communion of sorrows and of will between Mary and Christ, she merited to become ... the dispenser of all the benefits which Jesus acquired for us by His death and the shedding of His Blood."
~St. Pius X,
Encyclical, Ad Diem Illum

TABLE OF CONTENTS

FOREWORD

THE CHURCH'S HIGH ESTEEM FOR ST. ALPHONSUS LIGUORI

In order to properly convey to the reader the value of the writings of St. Alphonsus Liguori, following the example of the editors of the *Centenary Edition of the Works of St. Alphonsus*, I would like to present many of the statements of approval issued by the Church, in particular by numerous sovereign Pontiffs. The following is a summary of the Preface to the Centenary Edition, which is contained in the first volume of the Ascetical Works, in which the editors presented this inspiring information.

~~~

The writings of St. Alphonsus Liguori were praised both during his life as well as after his death. The learned Pope Benedict XIV, for example, "approved very highly of the writings of the Saint, and in a letter addressed to him in regard to his Moral Theology, expressed the belief that his work would prove most welcome and useful to the whole

Christian world." Pope Clement XIV, who had the special favor from Our Lord to be assisted at his death by St. Alphonsus himself,[1] had held, in his life, "the highest esteem for the Saint." The veneration felt for St. Alphonsus by the sovereign Pontiffs was such that Pope Pius VII desired to "to possess as relics the three fingers of the right hand with which the Saint had written his works and defended the honor of God, of the Blessed Virgin, and of our holy religion."

It was this same Pope who confirmed the judgment of the Sacred Congregation of Rites which, on May 3, 1803, had decreed that the printed and unprinted works of St. Alphonsus Liguori contained "nothing that deserves censure." Twelve years later, in 1815, Pope Pius VII further approved a decree of the same Congregation which highlighted the divine favors which had been bestowed upon St. Alphonsus. It stated that God had called St. Alphonsus "that he should shine by the light of apostolic virtues" as one of the "stars that ... shine in the firmament of the Church militant." Through his obedience to God's call and graces, St. Alphonsus, "like the sun that sends its rays everywhere, ... sent forth rays of virtues, worthy of an apostle, when he condemned the honors of the world or showed by his voice and his writings, the road of justice to those who were wandering about in the dark night of this world, that they might be able to pass from the power of darkness into the light and the kingdom of God; or when he gave the best rules to his disciples whom he called members of the Congregation of the Most Holy Redeemer; or when, as Bishop, he united fortitude to meekness, and adorned his crown with the ornaments of the other virtues like so many heavenly jewels."

By declaring him a Saint, the Congregation stated that this would be a cause of great joy for the Church. It would be an event in which the faithful would be inspired and reminded

---

[1] This is a wonderful story. St. Alphonsus, the greatest moral Doctor of the Church, also possessed many mystical gifts. Among them was the gift of bilocation in which he was able to be with the dying Pope at the moment of his death. This occurred in the context of an ecstasy when the Saint was at prayer, something he had experienced numerous times before.

that, though the world and the times change, the Church of Christ will never change nor perish, and "that the spirit of our holy Fathers has not become extinct; and that the Spouse of Christ never grows old, but amid the perishableness and changeableness of the years is ever blooming in continual youth and beauty."

Within the Bull of Beatification, pronounced by Pope Pius VII on September 6, 1816, we can read "the finest eulogy of Saint Alphonsus." The Holy Father said,

> Alphonsus was in God's hands a sharp arrow, which, discharged against vice, strikes now in one place, now in another, in order to promote the honor of God and the salvation of souls. As a sharp arrow, heated by the fire of love, he has wounded the hearts of not a few priests, and so inflamed them that they also left all things and followed their Redeemer. Thus he established the Congregation of the Most Holy Redeemer, whose priests have the special duty to preach to the people living scattered in the country. One cannot wonder enough how many enmities he has removed, how many wandering sinners he has led back to the right road and to Christian perfection, by word and example, and by his numerous writings. Besides, he was so devoted a client of the Mother of God, that it was always a pleasure to him to praise this sublime Mother and Virgin, and to write about her glories books filled with holy learning.[2] Bowed down physically by age, labor, and very grievous illness, yet mentally strong and ardent, he never ceased to speak and to write about heavenly things till his ninetieth year, when full of joy, he died a saintly death.

---

[2] In particular his book, *The Glories of Mary.*

In 1825, when he approved of the complete edition of the works of St. Alphonsus, Pope Leo XII said that the Saint was "among the number of pious and learned writers raised up by Divine Providence to stem the torrent of bad publications which at that time was rushing down on society." He said that within his works we find a "most tender piety and devotion, and ... singular zeal" which animates his voice urging the faithful to make frequent use of the Sacraments, instilling a love for Our Lord and a trust in His mercy, as well as a true devotion to Our Lady and to the saints, the latter being, Leo XII added, "indeed the surest bulwarks against every kind of demoralization."

Pope Pius VIII, even as a Cardinal, gave evidence of "his great affection for Saint Alphonsus." He praised the Bishop of Marseilles for his efforts to promote among the faithful a veneration for St. Alphonsus, stating that the Saint "has adorned the august episcopate with the lustre of his virtues," and has "made it resplendent by a doctrine that is sound and according to God (*sana ac secundum Deum*)." Further, on another occasion, Pius VIII said that St. Alphonsus "was conspicuous by the light of all the virtues that can be imitated by the clergy, and his writings are a pure fountain (*fons purus*), from which one may draw sacred science without endangering the piety of faith, as Saint Jerome expresses himself."

Gregory XVI, in praise of "the profound learning and eminent sanctity of Saint Alphonsus," said that the Saint was "resplendent even among the brilliant lights that adorn the Catholic Church." It was this Pope who placed the name of St. Alphonsus in the ecclesiastical calendar and extended his feast to the universal Church. Gregory XVI also oversaw the decision to declare that, regarding the writings of St. Alphonsus, since "there is nothing found worthy of censure, the opinions of Saint Alphonsus may be followed in the pulpit as well as in the confessional, even if one has not maturely examined the reasons upon which the opinions are founded."[3]

The value of the writings of St. Alphonsus is a recurrent theme in the praises issued by the sovereign Pontiffs. In addition to what has already been presented, Pope Pius IX, in writing to the Saint's Order, the Congregation of the Most Holy Redeemer, on November 25, 1846, expressed "his joy and consolation on hearing that the German edition of the works of Saint Alphonsus had met with so great success." The reason for this joy was because it came "at a moment … when by the insidious devices of the enemies of religion so many pestilential books are in circulation on every side, to corrupt and deprave the minds and morals especially of those not on their guard against them."[4]

Reading his writings, this Holy Father added, "cannot but be of the greatest advantage, not only to Christians in general, but also to ecclesiastics, and to those especially who have the care and the direction of souls. For the works of that most holy and most learned man, written with an extraordinary tenderness of piety and devotion, breathe in every page a special love for Jesus Christ, and confidence in His merits and mercy; they inspire the highest devotion to the Virgin Mother of God and to the saints; they inflame men's hearts with the desire of frequenting the most holy Sacraments, and furnish a most copious supply of excellent admonitions, counsels, and injunctions for procuring and carrying on the work of the salvation of souls."

After hearing these rich praises of his holy writings, it is not surprising that it was this same Pope, Pius IX, "who graciously responded to the petition of many Cardinals,

---

[3] An example of how impressed the hierarchy was with St. Alphonsus Liguori can be seen in the fact that this declaration of Pope Gregory XVI "induced the Cardinal Archbishop of Besangon, Rohan-Chabot, earnestly to exhort his clergy to adhere to the practice of Saint Alphonsus, in order that uniformity might be attained."

[4] This is another reason why the effort of bringing forth the writings of this great Saint are needed in our generation.

Patriarchs, Archbishops, Bishops, and other dignitaries"[5] and declared Saint Alphonsus to be a Doctor of the Church. Even more striking is the fact that, at that time, the Church had not bestowed this distinction on any ecclesiastical writer or theologian from the previous five centuries.[6]

Within the decree which placed him among the Doctors of the Church, we find further examples of the Church's high regard for St. Alphonsus Liguori:

> Among those who have done and taught, and whom our Lord Jesus Christ has declared should be great in the kingdom of heaven, is rightly counted Saint Alphonsus Maria di Liguori, Founder of the Congregation of the Most Holy Redeemer, and Bishop of Saint Agatha of the Goths. He shone as a watch-light on its tower, giving examples of all virtues to those who follow Christ and are of the household of God. Already, because of the brightness of his light, he has been reckoned among the Saints, the domestics of God. But what he reduced to practice in his holy life, he taught also in word and by writing. He stands distinguished for exposing and destroying the lurking- places of unbelievers and Jansenists, so widely spread about. And, over and beyond this, he has cleared up questions that were clouded; he has solved what was doubtful, making a safe path, through which the

---

[5] The decree established him as a Doctor of the Church added: "Very many cardinals of the Holy Roman Church, almost all the prelates of the whole Catholic universe, the generals of religious orders, the theological faculties of the most celebrated universities, illustrious chapters of canons and learned men of every ecclesiastical body, have presented petitions to our Holy Father Pius IX, Supreme Pontiff, in which they express their common desires that Saint Alphonsus Maria di Liguori may be adorned with the title and the honors of *Doctor of the Church.*"

[6] The Saint who was declared a Doctor of the Church and who lived the closest in time to St. Alphonsus died in 1274, over five centuries earlier.

directors of Christian souls may tread with foot unhurt, between the involved opinions of theologians, whether too loose or too rigorous.

And besides this, he has signally cast light on the doctrines of the Immaculate Conception, and of the Infallibility of the Sovereign Pontiff teaching *ex cathedra*; and he strenuously taught these doctrines, which in our day have been defined as of faith.

He has, finally, made clear dark passages of the Holy Scriptures, both in his ascetic writings, which are freighted with a celestial odor, and in a most salutary commentary, in which, for the nourishment of piety and the instruction of the soul, he has given expositions of the Psalms, as well as of the hymns recited in the Divine Office, for the benefit especially of those obliged to its recitation.

Finally, from the original Preface to the Centenary Edition is included a letter from Pope Leo XIII to priests of the Congregation of the Most Holy Redeemer. In this, the Holy Father highlights how practical and approachable are the writings of St. Alphonsus. He said, "⌈St. Alphonsus⌉ very well knew how to adapt Catholic truths to the comprehension of all, to provide for the moral direction of souls, to excite in a wonderful way true piety in the hearts of all … He has by means of numerous learned ascetical works enkindled, as it were, by burning coals, nourished and augmented languishing love principally toward our Lord Jesus Christ and His sweetest Mother, for whom, to the great advantage of the people, he knew how to inflame the coldest hearts." As a result, and, as he emphasized, "what is above all worthy of remark, though he wrote so many things, it must be acknowledged that, after an attentive examination, these writings may be read by the faithful without the least danger to their faith." Therefore, the Holy Father added, "Although the writings of the holy Doctor Alphonsus Maria de Liguori have already been spread throughout the world, not without very great profit to the Christian religion, yet it is desirable that they be propagated more and more, and be found in the hands of all."

~~~

It is for the latter reason, and for the reason of the manifold errors spread throughout the world today, as in the time of St. Alphonsus himself, that the works of St. Alphonsus must become known and read once again. Their orthodoxy, clarity, and accessibility, and their power to ignite within souls a great zeal for sanctity, make them invaluable gifts from Divine Providence. May this age of the world take them up and, by meditating on the eternal truths found in the school of this great Doctor, obtain their salvation and store up for themselves abundant treasures in Heaven.

The following presentation of *Our Lady of Sorrows* is comprised of sections taken from *The Glories of Mary*. The section on the *Sacramentals in Honor of Our Lady of Sorrows* is the only one composed by me; all others, except the selections from the Encyclical of Pope St. Pius X, are those of St. Alphonsus Liguori. The only changes that have been made to the original involve very occasional punctuation and minor textual errors. Footnotes added by this publisher are marked "-SDP." Footnotes that end with "- Ed" are original to the Centenary Edition. The writings of St. Alphonsus contain, in the footnotes, the Latin text for all Scripture verses and books cited, which he typically also quotes within the text itself. These are retained in this edition for the aid of those who desire to delve further into the primary sources he utilized. The Latin text is from the Vulgate edition of the Bible, a greatly revered translation which the Church has relied upon since the time of St. Jerome.

Charles D. Fraune

PETITION OF ST. ALPHONSUS LIGUORI TO JESUS & MARY

My most loving Redeemer and Lord Jesus Christ, I thy poor servant, knowing how pleasing to thee are those who seek to glorify thy most holy mother, whom thou lovest so much, and dost so much desire to see loved and honored by all men, I propose to publish this book of mine which treats of her glories.[1] I know not to whom I could commend it but to thee, who hast so much at heart the glory of this mother. To thee, then, I present and dedicate it. Receive this little offering of my love for thee and thy beloved mother. Take it under thy protection, and pour into the hearts of those who read it the light of confidence in this immaculate Virgin, and the warmth of a burning love for her, in whom thou hast placed the hope and refuge of all the redeemed. And for the reward of this, my poor effort, give me, I pray thee, that love for Mary with which I have desired to inflame, by this my little work, the hearts of all those who read it.

---

[1] This section was written by St. Alphonsus Liguori for the publication of *The Glories of Mary*.

To thee also I appeal, oh my sweetest Lady and mother Mary. Thou knowest that in thee, next to Jesus, I have placed all hope of my eternal salvation, since all the good I have received, my conversion, my vocation to leave the world, and whatever other graces have been given me by God, I acknowledge them all as coming through thee. Thou knowest that to see thee loved by all as thou dost deserve, and to offer thee some token of gratitude, I have always sought to proclaim thee everywhere, in public and in private, and to inspire all men with a sweet and salutary devotion to thee. I hope to continue to do so for the remainder of my life, even to my last breath. But I see by my advanced age and declining health that the end of my pilgrimage and my entrance into eternity are drawing near; therefore, I hope to give to the world, before my death, this little book of mine which may continue to proclaim thee for me, and also may excite others to publish thy glories and the great mercy which thou dost exercise towards thy devoted servants. I hope, my most beloved queen, that this my poor offering, although it falls so far short of thy merit, may be pleasing to thy grateful heart, since it is wholly a gift of love. Extend, then, that most kind hand of thine with which thou hast delivered me from the world and from hell, and accept it and protect it as belonging to thee. But I ask this reward for my little offering, that henceforth I may love thee more, and that all into whose hands this work shall fall, may be inflamed with thy love, so that immediately their desire may increase to love thee, and see others love thee also; and that they may engage with all ardor in proclaiming and promoting, as far as possible, thy praise, and confidence in thy most holy intercession. Thus I hope, thus may it be.

TO THE READER

In order that this little work of mine may not be exposed to censure from very fastidious critics, I have thought it best to place in a clearer light some of the propositions which it contains, and which may seem too bold, or perhaps obscure.[1] I here enumerate some of them, and if others, my dear reader, should come under your eye, I pray you to consider them as meant and spoken by me according to the sense of true and sound theology, and of the holy Roman Catholic Church, whose obedient son I profess myself. In the introduction, ... referring to the fifth chapter of the book, I have said that God has ordained that all graces should come to us through the hands of Mary. Now this is a very consoling truth for souls tenderly attached to the most holy Mary, and for poor sinners who desire to be converted. Nor should this appear to any one inconsistent with sound theology, since its author, St. Augustine, puts it forth as a general statement, that Mary has

---

[1] This section was written by St. Alphonsus Liguori for the publication of *The Glories of Mary*.

shared, by means of her charity, in the spiritual birth of all the members of the Church.[2]

A well-known author, whom no one will suspect of exaggeration or of fanciful and overheated devotion, adds, that as Jesus Christ really formed his Church on Calvary, it is plain that the holy Virgin really co-operated with him, in a peculiar and excellent manner, in its formation.[3] And for the same reason it may be said, that if she brought forth Jesus Christ, the head of the Church, without pain, she did not bring forth the body of this head without pain. Hence she commenced on Calvary to be, in a particular manner, mother of the whole Church. To say all in a few words, Almighty God, in order to glorify the mother of the Redeemer, has ordained that her great charity should intercede for all those for whom her divine Son offered and paid the superabundant ransom of his precious blood, in which alone is our *salvation, life, and resurrection.*

It is on the basis of this doctrine and whatever belongs to it that I have undertaken to establish my propositions,[4] which the saints in their affecting colloquies with Mary, and in their fervent discourses concerning her, have not hesitated to assert: when an ancient father, quoted by the celebrated Vincenzo Contensone, has written: The fulness of grace was in Christ as the head from which it flows, but in Mary as the neck through which it is transmitted.[5] This is plainly taught by the angelic Doctor, St. Thomas, who confirms all the foregoing in these words: The blessed Virgin is called full of grace in three ways ... The third, in reference to its

---

[2] Mater quidem spiritu non capitis nostri, quod est ipse salvator, ex quo magis illa spiritualiter nata est; quia omnes, qui in eum crediderint, in quibus et ipsa est, recte filii sponsi appellantur; sed plane mater membrorum ejus (quae nos sumus) quia cooperata est charitate, ut fideles in Ecclesia nascerentur, qui illius capitis membra sunt. Lib. de Sancta Virginitate, cap. 6.

[3] M. Nicole, Instr. theol. and mor. on the Lord's Prayer, the Angelical Salutation, &c, Instr. 5, c. 2.

[4] Part 1, c. 6, § 2, c. 7, 8, § 2, c. 9.

[5] In Christo fuit plenitudo gratiae, sicut in capite influente, in Maria vero, sicut in collo transfundente. Theolog. mentis et cordis. Tom. 2, Lib. 10. Dissert. 6, c. 1. Speculat. 2. in Reflexiones.

overflowing upon all men. For great is it in each saint if he hath enough of grace for the salvation of many; but this would be the greatest, if he had enough for the salvation of all men; and it is so with Christ and the blessed Virgin, for in every danger we may obtain salvation through the glorious Virgin. Hence, cant. 4, v. 4, *a thousand bucklers* – that is, remedies against dangers – hang upon her: *"Mille clypei pendent ex ea."* Hence in every virtuous work we can have her aid, and, therefore, she herself says, In me is all hope of life and of virtue: "In me omnis spes vitae et virtutis."[6]

---

[6] Dicitur autem Beata Virgo plena gratiae, quantum ad tria . . .Tertio quo ad refusionem in omnes homines. Magnum enim est in quolibet sancto, quando habet tantum de gratia quod sufficit ad salutem multorum; sed quando haberet tantum, quod sufficeret ad salutem omnium hominum de mundo, hoc esset maximum; et hoc est in Christo et in Beata Virgine. Nam in omni periculo potes salutem obtinere ab ipsa Virgine gloriosa. Unde cantic. 4. *Mille clypei,* id est remedia contra pericula, *pendent ex ea.* Item in omni opere virtutis potes eam habere in adjutorium: et ideo dicit ipsa. Eccli. xxiv. 25

INTRODUCTION WHICH OUGHT TO BE READ

My dear reader and brother in Mary, since the devotion which has urged me to write, and now moves you to read this book[1], renders us both happy children of this good mother, if you ever should hear any one say that I could have spared this labor, there being so many learned and celebrated books that treat of this subject, answer him, I pray you, in the words of Francone the abbot, which we find in the Library of the Fathers, that the praise of Mary is a fountain so full that the more it extends, the fuller it becomes, and the fuller it becomes the more it extends;[2] which signifies that the blessed Virgin is so great and sublime, that the more we praise her, the more there is to praise. So that St. Augustine says: All the tongues of men, even if all their members were changed to

---

[1] This section was written by St. Alphonsus Liguori for the publication of *The Glories of Mary*.
[2] Laus Mariae fons est indeficiens, qui quanto amplius tenditur, tanto amplius impletur; quanto amplius impletur, tanto amplius dilatatur.

tongues, would not be sufficient to praise her as she deserves.[3]

I know that there are innumerable books, both great and small, which treat of the glories of Mary; but as these are rare or voluminous, and not according to my plan, I have endeavored to collect in a small space, from all the authors at my command, the most select and pithy sentences of the Fathers and theologians, in order to give devout persons an opportunity, with little effort or expense, to inflame their ardor by reading of the love of Mary, and especially, to present materials to priests which may enable them to excite by their sermons devotion to the divine mother.

Worldly lovers are accustomed to mention frequently and to praise the persons beloved, that these may be praised and applauded also by others; then how poor must we suppose the love of those to be who boast of being lovers of Mary, but who seldom remember to speak of her, and inspire the love of her also in others! Not so the true lovers of our most lovely Lady: they would praise her everywhere, and see her loved by all the world; and therefore in public and in private, wherever it is in their power, they endeavor to kindle in the hearts of all, those blessed flames of love with which theirs are burning for their beloved queen.

But that every one may be persuaded of how great benefit it is to himself and the people to promote devotion to Mary, let us hear what the Fathers say of it. St. Bonaventure declares that those who are devoted to publishing the glories of Mary, are secure of paradise; and Richard of St. Laurence confirms this by saying, that to honor the queen of angels is to acquire life everlasting;[4] since our most grateful Lady, adds the same author, pledges herself to honor in the other life him who promises to honor her in this;[5] and is there any one ignorant of the promise made by Mary herself to those

_____

[3] Etiamsi omnium nostrum membra verterentur in linguas eam laudare sufficiret nullus. Ap. B. Dion. Carth.

[4] Honorare Mariam est thesaurizare vitam eternam. De Laud. v. c. 2.

[5] Honorificantes se in hoc saeculo honorificabit in futuro.

8

who engage in promoting the knowledge and love of her upon the earth? "They that explain me shall have life everlasting,"[6] as the holy Church applies it on the festival of her Immaculate Conception. Exult, exult! oh my soul! said St. Bonaventure, who was so assiduous in proclaiming the praises of Mary, and rejoice in her, because many good things are prepared for those who praise her; and since all the Holy Scriptures, he added, speak in praise of Mary, let us endeavor always with heart and tongue to celebrate this our divine mother, that we may be conducted by her to the kingdom of the blessed.[7]

We are told in the revelations of St. Bridget, that the blessed Emingo, Bishop, being accustomed to begin his sermons with the praises of Mary, the Virgin herself appeared one day to the saint, and said to her: "Tell that prelate who is accustomed to commence his discourses with my praises, that I will be his mother, and that I will present his soul to God, and that he shall die a good death;"[8] and he indeed died like a saint, in prayer and in celestial peace. Mary appeared before his death to another religious, a Dominican, who was accustomed to terminate his sermons by speaking of her. She defended him from the assaults of the demons, comforted him, and bore away with her his happy soul.[9]

The devout Thomas à Kempis represents Mary as commending to her Son those who publish her praise, and saying, "Oh, my Son, have compassion on the souls of thy lovers, and of those who speak in my praise."[10]

As far as the advantage of the people is concerned, St. Anselm says, that the sacred womb of Mary having been made the way of salvation for sinners, sinners cannot but be

---

[6] Qui elucidant me, vitam eternam habebunt. Eccli. xxiv, 31.
[7] Exulta, exulta, anima mea, et laetare in illa; quia multa bona sunt laudatoribus praeparata. Si enim omnes scripturae loquuntur de ea, Deiparam perpetuo corde et lingua celebremus, ut ab ipsa ad gaudia eterna perducamur.
[8] Revel. cap. 14.
[9] Ap. P. Auriem.
[10] Fili miserere animae amatoris tui et laudutoris mei. Serm. 20, ad Nov.

converted and saved by discourses in praise of Mary.[11] If the assertion is true and incontrovertible, as I believe it to be, and as I shall prove, in the fifth chapter of this book,[12] that all graces are dispensed by the hand of Mary alone, and that all those who are saved, are saved solely by means of this divine mother; it may be said, as a necessary consequence, that the salvation of all depends upon preaching Mary, and confidence in her intercession. We know that St. Bernard of Sienna sanctified Italy; St. Dominic converted many provinces; St. Louis Bertrand, in all his sermons, never failed to exhort his hearers to practise devotion towards Mary; and many others also have done the same.

I find that Father Paul Segneri, the younger, a celebrated missionary, in every mission preached a sermon on devotion to Mary, and this he called his favorite sermon. And we can attest, in all truth, that in our missions, where we have an invariable rule not to omit the sermon on our Lady, no discourse is so profitable to the people, or excites more compunction among them, than that on the mercy of Mary. I say *on the mercy of Mary:* for St. Bernard says, we may praise her humility, and marvel at her virginity; but being poor sinners, we are more pleased and attracted by hearing of her mercy; for to this we more affectionately cling, this we more often remember and invoke.[13] Therefore in this little book, leaving to other authors the description of the other merits of Mary, I have confined myself especially to treating of her great compassion and her powerful intercession; having collected, as far as possible, with the labor of years, all that the holy Fathers and the most celebrated authors have said of the mercy and power of Mary; and because these attributes of the blessed Virgin are wonderfully set forth in the great

---

[11] Quomodo fieri potest ut ex memoria laudum ejus salus nos proveniat peccatorum, cujus uterus facta est via ad peccatores salvandos? S. Ans. Lib. 8, de Exc. V. cap. l.

[12] The Glories of Mary

[13] Laudamus humilitatem, miramur virginitatem; sed miseris sapit dulcius misericordia; misericordiam amplectimur carius, recordamur saepius, crebrius invocamus. Serm. 4, de Ass.

prayer of the Salve Regina, approved by the Church and required by her to be recited the greater part of the year by all the clergy, secular and regular, I have undertaken, in the first place, to explain in separate discourses this most devout prayer. Besides this, I believed it would be acceptable to the servants of Mary, if I added discourses on her principal festivals and upon the virtues of our divine mother, placing at the conclusion of them the practices of devotion most in use among her servants, and approved by the Church.

Devout reader, if this little work of mine pleases you, as I hope it will, I pray you to commend me to the Holy Virgin, that I may obtain great confidence in her protection. Ask for me this grace, and I will ask the same for you, who ever you may be, who bestow on me this charity. Oh, blessed is he who clings with love and confidence to those two anchors of salvation, Jesus and Mary! He certainly will not be lost. Let us both say, oh my reader, with the devout Alphonso Rodriguez: Jesus and Mary, my sweet loves, for you I will suffer, for you I will die; may I be wholly yours, may I be in nothing my own.[14] May we love Jesus and Mary, and become saints, since we can aspire and hope for no greater happiness than this. Farewell, till we meet in heaven at the feet of this sweet mother and her dearly beloved Son, to praise them, to thank them, and love them, in their immediate presence through all eternity. Amen.

---

[14] Jesus et Maria, amores mei dulcissimi, pro vobis patiar, pro nobis moriar; sim totus vester, sim nihil meus. Ap. Auriem Aff. sc.

Discourse On the Dolors of Mary

Discourse IX
From *The Glories of Mary*

Mary was Queen of martyrs, because her martyrdom was longer and greater than that of all the martyrs.

Who can have a heart so hard that it will not melt on hearing of a most lamentable event which once happened in the world? There was a noble and holy mother who had but one only Son; and he was the most amiable that could be imagined, innocent, virtuous, beautiful, and most loving towards his mother; so much so, that he never had caused her the least displeasure, but always had showed her all respect, obedience, and affection. Hence the mother had placed on this Son all her earthly affections. Now what happened? It happened that this Son, through envy, was falsely accused by his enemies, and the judge, although he knew and confessed his innocence, yet, that he might not offend his enemies, condemned him to an infamous death, precisely as they had requested him to do. And this poor mother had to suffer the affliction of seeing that amiable and beloved Son so unjustly taken from her, in the flower of his age, by a barbarous death; for he was made to die in torment, drained of his blood before her own eyes in a public place, upon an infamous gibbet.

Devout souls, what do you say? Is this case and this unhappy mother worthy of compassion? Already you know of whom I speak. This Son so cruelly slain was our loving Redeemer, Jesus, and his mother was the blessed Virgin Mary, who, for love of us, was willing to see him offered up to the divine justice by the barbarity of men. This great pain, then, which Mary suffered for us – a pain which was more than a thousand deaths – merits our compassion and gratitude. And if we can return nothing else for so much love, at least let us for a little time today stop to consider the severity of the suffering by which Mary became Queen of martyrs; for her great martyrdom exceeded in suffering that of all the martyrs, being, in the first place the longest martyrdom; and in the second place, the greatest martyrdom.

First Point

As Jesus is called King of sorrows and King of martyrs, because he suffered in his life more than all the other martyrs, so is also Mary called, with reason, Queen of the martyrs, having merited this title by suffering the greatest martyrdom that could be suffered, next to that of her Son. Hence, she was justly named by Richard of St. Laurence the martyr of martyrs: "Martyr martyrum." And to her may be applied what Isaias said: *He will crown thee with the crown of tribulation*: "Coronans coronabit te tribulatione." For that suffering itself which exceeded the suffering of all the other martyrs united, was the crown by which she was shown to be the Queen of martyrs. That Mary was a true martyr cannot be doubted, as is proved by the Carthusian, Pelbart, Catharinus, and others; for it is an established opinion that suffering sufficient to cause death constitutes martyrdom, although death may not then take place. St. John the Evangelist is revered as a martyr, although he did not die in the caldron of boiling oil, but came out more sound than he went in: "Vegetior exiverit quam intraverit."[1] It is sufficient to procure the glory of

---

[1] Brev. Rom. 6, Maj.

martyrdom, says St. Thomas, that any one should be obedient even to offer himself to death.[2] Mary was a martyr, says St. Bernard, not by the sword of the executioner, but by the bitter sorrow of her heart.[3] If her body was not wounded by the hand of the executioner, yet her blessed heart was pierced by grief at the passion of her Son; a grief sufficient to cause her not only one, but a thousand deaths. And from this we shall see that Mary was not only a true martyr, but that her martyrdom surpassed that of all the other martyrs, for it was a longer martyrdom, and, if I may thus express it, all her life was a long death.

The passion of Jesus commenced with his birth, as St. Bernard says;[4] and Mary also, in all things like unto her Son, suffered her martyrdom through her whole life. The name of Mary, among its other significations, as the blessed Albertus Magnus affirms, signifies a *bitter sea*: "Mare amarum." Wherefore to her is applied the passage of Jeremias: *Great as the sea is thy destruction*: "Magna est enim velut mare contritio tua."[5] For as the sea is all salt and bitter, thus the life of Mary was always full of bitterness, at the sight of the passion of the Redeemer, which was ever present to her. It cannot be doubted that being more enlightened by the Holy Spirit than all the prophets, she better comprehended than they the predictions concerning the Messias, which they recorded in their holy Scriptures. Precisely this the angel revealed to St. Bridget.[6] Whence, as the same angel declared, the Virgin knowing how much the incarnate Word was to suffer for the salvation of men, even before she became his mother, and compassionating this innocent Saviour, who was to be so

---

[2] Martyrium amplectitur id quod in obedientia summum esse potest, ut scilicet aliquis sit obediens usque ad mortem. 2, 2, q. 134, a. 3, ad 3.

[3] Non ferro carnificis, sed acerbo dolore cordis. Ap. Baldi. tom.1, p. 146

[4] A nativitatis exordio, passio crucis simul exorta. Serm. 2, de Pass.

[5] Thr. ii. 13.

[6] Proculdubio est credendum, quod ipsa ex inspiratione Spiritus Sancti perfectius intellexit quicquid Prophetarum eloquia figurabant. Serm. Ang. c. 17.

cruelly put to death for crimes not his own, she commenced, from that time, her great martyrdom.[7]

Her grief afterwards increased immeasurably when she was made mother of this Saviour. So that at the painful thought of all the sufferings which her poor Son was to endure, she indeed experienced, says Rupert the Abbot, a long martyrdom – a martyrdom continued through her whole life.[8] And exactly this was signified by the vision which St. Bridget had at Rome, in the Church of St. Mary Major, where the blessed Virgin appeared to her with St. Simeon, and an angel, having a sword which was very long and red with blood; by which was prefigured the long and bitter grief that pierced the heart of Mary during her whole life.[9] Whence the above-named Rupert puts into the mouth of Mary the following words: Oh, redeemed souls and my beloved children, do not pity me only for that hour in which I saw my dear Jesus dying in my presence, for the sword of sorrow, predicted to me by Simeon, pierced my soul during my whole life; when I was giving suck to my Son, when I was warming him in my arms, I already saw the bitter death that awaited him; consider then what long and cruel sorrows I must have endured.[10]

Wherefore Mary might truly say in the words of David: "My life is wasted with grief and my years in sighs.[11] My sorrow is continually before me: 'Dolor meus in conspectu meo semper.'[12] My life was wholly passed in grief and tears; for my grief, which was compassion for my beloved Son, never departed from before my eyes, seeing, as I did

---

[7] Ex Scripturis Deum incarnari intelligens, et quod tam diversis poenis deberet cruciari, tribulationem non modicam sustinuit. Serm. Ang. c. 16.

[8] Tu longum praescia futurae passionis filii tui, pertulisti martyrium. In Cant. c. 4.

[9] Rev. 1. 7, c. 2.

[10] Nolite solam attendere horam illam qua dilectum meum vidi mori; nam Simeonis gladius, antequam pertransiret, longum per me transitum fecit. Cum igitur eum lactarem, foverem et prospicerem ejus mortem, quam prolixam me putatis pertulisse passionem? Loc. cit.

[11] Defecit in dolore vita mea, et anni mei in gemitibus. Psal. xxx. 11.

[12] Psal. xxxvii. 18.

continually, the sufferings and death that he was one day to endure." The divine mother herself revealed to St. Bridget, that even after the death and ascension of her Son into heaven, the memory of his passion, whether she ate or worked, was deeply impressed and ever recent in her tender heart.[13] Taulerus therefore says, that Mary passed her whole life in perpetual sorrow; for her heart was always occupied with thoughts of sadness and of suffering.[14]

So that time, which usually mitigates the sorrows of the afflicted, did not relieve Mary; nay, time itself increased her sorrow, for as Jesus increased in years, on the one hand, he continually showed himself more lovely and amiable; and on the other, the time of his death was ever drawing nearer, and grief at having to lose him on this earth, continually increased in the heart of Mary. As the rose grows up among thorns, said the angel to St. Bridget, so the mother of God advanced in years in the midst of sufferings; and as the thorns increase with the growth of the rose, thus this rose selected by the Lord, Mary, as she increased in age, was so much the more pierced by the thorns of her dolors.[15] Having considered the length of this suffering, let us now pass on to the second point, namely, the consideration of its greatness.

Second Point

Ah, Mary was not only queen of the martyrs, because her martyrdom was longer than that of all others, but also because it was the greatest of all. But who can measure its greatness? Jeremias appears to be unable to find any one with whom he may compare this mother of sorrows, when

---

[13] Tempore quo post ascensionem filii mei vixi, passio sua in corde meo fixa erat, ut sive comedebam, sive laborabam, quasi recens erat in memoria mea. Rev. 1. 6, c. 65.

[14] Beatissima Virgo pro tota vita fecit professionem doloris. Vit. Christ. c 28.

[15] Sicut rosa crescere solet inter spinas ita B. Virgo in hoc mundo crevit inter tribulationes; et sicut, crescente rosa, crescunt spinae; sic haec electissima rosa Maria, quanto crescebat aetate, tanto tribulationum spinis pungebatur. Serm. Aug. c. 16.

considering her great suffering at the death of her Son. "To what shall I compare thee, or to what shall I liken thee, oh daughter of Jerusalem; for great as the sea is thy destruction; who shall heal thee?"[16] Wherefore Cardinal Hugo, commenting on these words, says: Oh blessed Virgin, as the bitterness of the sea exceeds all other bitterness, so thy grief surpasses all other griefs.[17] Hence St. Anselm affirms, that if God, by a special miracle, had not preserved the life of Mary, her grief would have been sufficient to cause her death at each moment of her life.[18] And St. Bernardine of Sienna even says that the grief of Mary was so great, that if it were divided among all men, it would be enough to cause their immediate death.[19]

But let us consider the reasons why the martyrdom of Mary was greater than that of all the martyrs. In the first place, it must be remembered that the martyrs suffered their martyrdom in the body, by means of fire or steel; Mary suffered martyrdom in her soul; as St. Simeon had before prophesied: and thy own soul a sword shall pierce: "Et tuam ipsius animam pertransibit gladius:"[20] as if the holy old man had said to her: Oh holy Virgin, the bodies of the other martyrs will be torn with iron, but thou wilt be pierced and martyred in thy soul, by the passion of thy own Son. Now, as the soul is more noble than the body, so much greater was the suffering of Mary than that of all the martyrs; as Jesus Christ himself said to St. Catharine of Sienna: There is no comparison between the sufferings of the soul and the body; "Inter dolorem animae et corporis nulla est comparatio." Whence the holy Abbot Arnold Carnotensis says that whoever had been present on Calvary at the great sacrifice of

---

[16] Cui comparabo te? vel cui assimilabo te, filia Jerusalem? Magna est enim velut mare contritio tua. Quis medebitur tui? Thren. ii. 1. (Lamentations)

[17] Quemadmodum mare est in amaritudine excellens, ita tuae contritioni nulla calamitas aequari potest.

[18] Utique, Domina, non erediderim te potuisse stimulos tanti cruciatus, quin vitam amitteres, sustinere; nisi ipse spiritus tui filii te confortaret. De Ec. Virg. c. 3.

[19] Tantua fuit dolor Virginis, quod si inter omnes creaturas, quae dolorem pati possunt, divideretur, omnes subito interirent. To. 1, Serm. 67.

[20] Luke 2:35

the immaculate Lamb, when he was dying on the cross, would have there beheld two great altars, one in the body of Jesus, the other in the heart of Mary: for there, at the same time that the Son sacrificed his body in death, Mary sacrificed her soul in compassion.[21]

Moreover, while the other martyrs, St. Antoninus says,[22] suffered by sacrificing their own lives, the blessed Virgin suffered by sacrificing the life of her Son, whom she loved far more than her own life; so that she not only suffered in spirit all that her Son suffered in body, but, moreover, the sight of the sufferings of her Son brought more grief to her heart than if she had endured them all in her own person. There can be no doubt that Mary suffered in her heart all the tortures by which she saw her beloved Jesus tormented. Every one knows that the sufferings of children are also the sufferings of their mothers, when they are the witnesses of them. St. Augustine, considering the anguish that the mother of the Macchabees experienced in witnessing the tortures which her sons endured, says: "She suffered in them all, because she loved them all, and endured with her eyes what they all endured in the flesh."[23] Thus also was it with Mary; all those scourgings, torments, thorns, nails, and the cross, which tortured the innocent flesh of Jesus, entered at the same time into the heart of Mary to complete her martyrdom. He in the flesh, she in the heart, suffered, writes St. Amadeus: "Ille carne, illa corde passa est."[24] So that as St. Lawrence Justinian says, the heart of Mary became as it were, a mirror of the agonies of her Son, in which were seen the spitting, the scourging, the wounds, and all that Jesus suffered.[25] And St. Bonaventure remarks, that these wounds which were

---

[21] Nimirum in tabernaculo illo duo videres altaria, aliud in pectore matris, aliud in corpore Christi; Christus carnem, Maria immolabat animam. Tr. de sep. verb. Do. in Cru.

[22] P. 1, tit. 15, c. 24.

[23] Illa videndo in omnibus passa est: quia amabat omnes, ferebat in oculis quod in carne omnes. Serm. 109, de Divers c. 6

[24] Hom. 5

[25] Passionis Christi speculum effectum erat cor Virginis, in illo agnoscebantur sputa, convicta, verbera, vulnera. De Agon. Chri. c. 11.

scattered all over the body of Jesus, were all united in one heart of Mary.[26]

The Virgin, then through compassion for her Son, was scourged, crowned with thorns, insulted, and nailed to the cross. Whence the same saint considering Mary on Mt. Calvary, where she was present with her dying Son, asks of her: "Oh Lady, tell me where you then stood? Perhaps only at the foot of the cross! Might I not rather say: thou wast on the cross itself crucified with thy Son?"[27] And Richard, remarking on the words of the Redeemer, which he spoke by the mouth of Isaias: "I have trodden the wine-press alone, and of the Gentiles there is not a man with me,"[28] adds: Oh Lord, thou dost rightly say that in the work of human redemption thou didst suffer alone, and there was no man that could pity thee sufficiently; but there was a woman with thee, thy own mother, who suffered in her heart whatever thou didst suffer in thy body.[29]

But all this is saying only too little of the sorrows of Mary; for, as I have before said, she suffered more in seeing her beloved Jesus suffer, than if in her own person she had endured all the tortures and the death of her Son. Erasmus has written, speaking of parents, generally, that they feel the sufferings of their children more than their own. But this is not always true. It was no doubt true of Mary, for she certainly loved her Son and his life far more than herself, and a thousand lives of her own.[30] Therefore St. Amadeus well declares that the afflicted mother, at the sorrowful sight of the agony of her beloved Jesus, suffered much more than if she herself had endured his whole passion.[31] The reason is

---

[26] Singula vulnera per ejus corpus dispersa, in uno corde sunt unita. De Planctu. Virg. in Stim. Am.

[27] O Domina mea ubi stabas? Nunquid tantum juxta crucem? Imo in cruce cum filio crucifixa eras. Loc. cit.

[28] Torcular calcavi solus, et de gentibus non est vir mecum. Isa. lxiii. 3.

[29] Verum est, Domine, quod non est vir tecum, sed mulier una est tecum, quae omnia vulnera quae tu suscepisti in corpore, suscepit in corde.

[30] Parentes atrocius torquentur in liberis, quam in seipsis. Libell. de Machab.

[31] Maria torquebatur magis, quam si torqueretur ex se; quoniam supra se incomparabiliter diligebat id unde dolebat. Cit. Horn, 5.

plain, since, as St. Bernard says: The soul is more where it loves, than where it lives: "Anima magis est ubi amat, quara ubi animat." And the Saviour himself had before said that our heart is where our treasure is.[32] If Mary, then, through love, lived more in her Son than in herself, a much greater grief did she suffer at the death of her Son, than if the most cruel death in the world had been inflicted on her.

And here is to be considered the other circumstance that rendered the martyrdom of Mary far greater than the sufferings of all the martyrs, for in the passion of Jesus she suffered much, and she suffered without alleviation. The martyrs suffered under the torments which their tyrants inflicted upon them, but love of Jesus rendered their pains sweet and delightful. A St. Vincent suffered in his martyrdom; he was tortured on the rack, torn with hooks, burnt with red-hot iron plates; but St. Augustine says: One seemed to suffer, and another to speak: "Alius videbatur pati, alias loqui." The saint addressed the tyrant with such power, and with such contempt of his torments, that it seemed as if one Vincent suffered and another Vincent spoke, so greatly did his God, with the sweetness of his love, comfort him in the midst of his sufferings. A St. Boniface suffered; his body was torn with irons, sharp-pointed reeds were thrust between his nails and flesh, melted lead was poured into his mouth, and at the same time he could not often enough repeat: I give thanks to thee, oh Jesus Christ: "Gratias tibi ago, Domine Jesu Christe." A St. Mark and a St. Marcellinus suffered; they were bound to a stake, their feet pierced by nails, and the tyrant appealed to them, saying: "Miserable beings, look at your condition, and save yourselves from these torments." And they answered: "What torments, what pain do you speak of? We have never feasted with more joy than now, when we are suffering with pleasure for the love of Jesus Christ."[33] A St. Lawrence suffered, but while he was

---

[32] Ubi thesaurus vester est, ibi et cor vestrum erit. Luc. xii. 34.
[33] Nunquam tarn jucunde epulati sumus, quam cum haec libenter Jesu Christi amore perferimus.

burning on the grid iron, the interior flames of love, as St. Leo says, was more powerful to cheer his soul, than the flames without were to torture his body.[34] Hence love made him so strong, that he even braved the tyrant by saying to him: Tyrant, if you wish to feed on my flesh, a part is sufficiently cooked, turn and eat: "Assatum est jam, versa et manduca." But in such torture and lingering death, how could the saint thus exult? Ah, St. Augustine answers, because, intoxicated with the wine of divine love, he felt neither torments nor death.[35]

For the holy martyrs, the more they loved Jesus, the less they felt torments and death, and the sight alone of the sufferings of a crucified God was sufficient to console them. But was not our afflicted mother, also, thus consoled by love for her Son, and the sight of his sufferings? No, for this very Son who suffered was the whole cause of her grief; and the love she bore him was her only, and too cruel, executioner; for the whole martyrdom of Mary consisted in seeing and pitying her innocent and beloved Son, who suffered so much. Therefore, the more she loved him, the more bitter and inconsolable was her sorrow. "Great as the sea is thy destruction, who shall heal thee?"[36] Ah, queen of heaven, love hath alleviated the sufferings of other martyrs, and has healed their wounds; but who has ever soothed thy great sorrow? Who has ever healed the cruel wounds of thy heart? Who will heal thee – "Quis medebitur tui?" – if that same Son, who could give thee consolation, was by his sufferings the sole cause of thy sorrows, and the love that thou didst bear him, caused all thy martyrdom? Therefore, whilst the other martyrs, as Diez remarks, are all represented with the instrument of their passion – St. Paul with the sword, St. Andrew with the cross, St. Lawrene with the gridiron – Mary is represented with her dead Son in her arms, because Jesus

---

[34] Segnior fuit ignis qui foris ussit, quam qui intus accendit. In. Nat. S. Laur.
[35] In illa longa naorte, in illis tormentis illo calice ebrius torments non sentit. Tract. 27.
[36] Magna est velut mare contritio tua; quis medebitur tui?

himself alone was the instrument of her martyrdom by reason of the love which she bore him. In a few words St. Bernard confirms all I have said: With the other martyrs their great love soothed the anguish of their martyrdom; but the more the blessed Virgin loved, so much the more she suffered, and so much more cruel was her martyrdom.[37]

It is certain that the greater is our love for a thing, the greater pain we feel in losing it. The loss of a brother certainly afflicts us more than the loss of a beast of burden; and the death of a son, more than that of a friend. Now Cornelius à Lapide says, that to comprehend how great was the grief of Mary at the death of her Son, we should comprehend how great was the love she bore him.[38] But who can measure that love? The blessed Amadeus says that in the heart of Mary two kinds of love to her Jesus were united: the supernatural love with which she loved him as her God, and the natural love with which she loved him as her son;[39] so that, of these two loves, one only was formed, but a love so immense that William of Paris even said, that the blessed Virgin loved Jesus to such a degree that a pure creature could not love him more.[40] And Richard of St. Laurence says, as there was no love like her love, so there was no grief like her grief.[41] If, therefore, the love of Mary for her Son was immense, immense also must have been her grief in losing him by death. Where love is greatest, says blessed Albertus Magnus, the grief is greatest: "Ubi summus amor, ibi summus dolor."

Let us imagine, then, that the divine mother, standing near her Son dying upon the cross, and justly applying to herself the words of Jeremias, says to us: "Oh, all ye that pass

---

[37] In aliis martyribus magnitudo amoris dolorem lenivit passionis; sed beata Virgo quanto plus amavit, tanto plus doluit tantoque ipsius martyrium gravius fuit. Ap. Crois. Vit. Mar. s. 23.

[38] Ut scias quantus fuerit dolor B. Virginis, cogita quantus fuerit amor.

[39] Duae dilectiones in unam convenerant et ex duobus amoribus factus est amor unus, cum Virgo mater filio divinitatis amorem impenderet, et in Deo amorem nato exhiberet. Hom. 5, de Laud. V.

[40] Quantum capere potuit puri hominis modus.

[41] Unde sicut non fuit amor sicut amor ejus, ita non fuit dolor sicut dolor ejus.

by the way attend, and see if there be any sorrow like to my sorrow."[42] "Oh ye that are passing your lives upon this earth, and have no pity for me, stop a while to look upon me, now that I behold that beloved Son dying before my eyes: and then see if among all who are afflicted and tormented, there be sorrow like to my sorrow." No, answers St. Bonaventure, there can be found no sorrow, oh afflicted mother, more bitter than thine, for no son can be found more dear than thine.[43] Ah, there has never been in the world, says St. Lawrence Justinian, a son more worthy of love than Jesus, nor a mother who loved her son more than Mary; if, then, there has never been in the world a love like the love of Mary, how can there be a grief like the grief of Mary?[44]

Therefore, St. Ildephonsus did not hesitate to affirm that it was little to say that the sufferings of the Virgin exceeded all the torments of the martyrs, even were they united together.[45] And St. Anselm adds, that the most cruel tortures inflicted upon the holy martyrs were light or nothing, in comparison with the martyrdom of Mary.[46] St. Basil likewise writes that as the sun surpasses in splendor all the other planets, so Mary in her sufferings exceeded the sufferings of all the other martyrs.[47] A certain learned author[48] concludes with an admirable sentiment, saying that so great was the sorrow which this tender mother suffered in the passion of Jesus, that she alone could worthily compassionate the death of a God made man.

---

[42] O vos omnes qui transitis per viam attendite et videte, si est dolor sicut dolor meus. Thren. i. 12.

[43] Nullus dolor amarior, quia nulla proles charior. De Compas. Virg. c. 2.

[44] Non fuit talis filius, non fuit talis mater; non fuit tanta charitas, non fuit dolor tantus. Ideo quanto dilexit tenerius, tanta vulnerata est profundius. Lib. 3, de Laud. Virg.

[45] Parum est Miriam in passione filii tam acerbos pertulisse dolores, ut omnium martyrum collective tormenta superaret. Ap. Sinisc. Mart. de Mar. Cons. 36.

[46] Quicquid crudelitatis inflictum est corporibus martyrum, leve fuit, aut potius nihil comparatione tuae passionis. De Exc. Virg. c. 5.

[47] Virgo universos martyres tantum excedit, quantum sol reliqua astra.

[48] P. Pinam.

But St. Bonaventure, addressing the blessed Virgin, says: Oh Lady, why hast thou wished to go and sacrifice thyself also on Calvary? Was not a crucified God sufficient to redeem us, that thou his mother wouldst be crucified also?[49] Indeed, the death of Jesus was more than enough to save the world, and also an infinity of worlds; but this good mother wished, for the love she bore us, likewise to aid the cause of our salvation with the merits of the sorrows which she offered for us on Calvary. And, therefore, says the blessed Albertus Magnus, as we are indebted to Jesus for what he suffered for love of us, we are also to Mary for the martyrdom which she, in the death of her Son, voluntarily suffered for our salvation.[50] I have added *voluntarily*, since, as the angel revealed to St. Bridget, this our so merciful and kind mother was willing to suffer any pain, rather than to see souls unredeemed or left in their former perdition.[51] It may be said that this was the only consolation of Mary in the midst of her great sorrow at the passion of her Son, to see the lost world redeemed by his death, and men, who were his enemies, reconciled with God. Grieving, she rejoiced, says Simon da Cassia, because the sacrifice was offered for the redemption of all, by which wrath was appeased.[52]

Such love as that of Mary merits our gratitude, and let us show our gratitude by meditating upon and compassionating her sorrows. But of this she complained to St. Bridget, that very few pitied her, and most lived forgetful of her sorrows. "I look around upon all who are in the world, if perchance there may be any to pity me, and meditate upon my sorrows, and truly I find very few. Therefore, my daughter, though I am forgotten by many, at least do not

---

[49] O Domina, cur ivisti immolari pro nobis? Non sufficiebat filii passio, nisi crucifigeretur et mater? Ap. Pac. Exc. 10, in Sal. Ang.

[50] Sicut totus mundus obligatur Deo propter passionem, sic obligatar Dominae propter compassionem. Sup. Miss. cap. 20.

[51] Sic pia et misericors est, et fuit, quod maluit omnes tribulationes sufferre, quam quod animae non redimerentur. Rev. 1. 3, c. 30.

[52] Laetabatur dolens quod offerebatur sacrificium in redemptionem omnium quo placabatur. De Gest. D. i. 2. c. 27.

thou forget me; behold my anguish, and imitate, as far as thou canst, my grief."[53] In order to understand how much the Virgin is pleased by our remembrance of her dolors, it is sufficient to relate, that in the year 1239, she appeared to seven of her servants, who then became the founders of the order of the Servants of Mary, with a black garment in her hand, and told them that if they wished to please her, they should often meditate upon her dolors; and therefore she wished, in memory of them, that they would hereafter wear that garment of mourning.[54] And Jesus Christ himself revealed to the blessed Veronica Binasco, that he takes more pleasure, as it were, in seeing his mother compassionated than himself; for thus he addressed her: "My daughter, the tears shed for my passion are dear to me; but loving with so great love my mother Mary, the meditation of the dolors which she suffered at my death is more dear to me."[55]

Wherefore the graces are very great which Jesus promises to those who are devoted to the dolors of Mary. Pelbart relates,[56] that it was revealed to St. Elizabeth, that St. John the Evangelist, after the blessed Virgin was assumed into heaven, desired to see her again. This favor was granted him; his dear mother appeared to him, and Jesus Christ with her; and he then heard Mary asking of her Son some peculiar grace for those who were devoted to her dolors; and Jesus promised her for them the four following special graces: *1st*: That those who invoke the divine mother by her sorrows will, before death, merit to obtain true repentance of all their sins. *2nd*: That he will protect such in their tribulations, especially at the hour of death. *3rd*: That he will impress upon them the memory of his passion, and that they shall have their reward for it in heaven. *4th*: That he will commit such

---

[53] Respicio ad omnes qui in mundo sunt, si forte sint aliqui qui compatiantur mihi, et recogitent dolorem meum; et valde paucos invenio. Ideo filia mea, licet a multis oblita sim, tu tamen non obliviscaris mei, vide dolorem meum, et imitare quam tum potes, et dole. Rev. 1.2, c. 24.

[54] Gian. Cent. Serv. 1. 1, c. 14

[55] Ap. Bolland. 13, Jan

[56] Stellar. 1. 3, p. 3, a. 3.

devout servants to the hands of Mary, that she may dispose of them according to her pleasure, and obtain for them all the graces she desires. In proof of this, let us see in the following example how devotion to the dolors of Mary may aid our eternal salvation.

EXAMPLE

We read in the revelations of St. Bridget,[57] that there was once a lord as noble by birth as he was low and sinful in his habits. He had given himself by an express compact as a slave to the devil, and had served him for sixty years, leading such a life as may easily be imagined, and never approaching the sacraments. Now, this prince was about to die and Jesus Christ, in his compassion, commanded St. Bridget to tell his confessor to visit him, and exhort him to make his confession. The confessor went, and the sick man told him that he had no need of a confessor, for that he had often made his confession. The confessor visited him a second time, and that poor slave of hell persevered in his obstinate determination not to make his confession. Jesus again directed the saint to tell the confessor to go to him again. He obeyed, and this third time related to him the revelation made to the saint, and that he had returned so many times because the Lord, who desired to show him mercy, had directed him to do so. On hearing this the dying man was moved, and began to weep. "But how," he exclaimed, "can I be pardoned, when for sixty years I have served the devil, made myself his slave, and have laden my soul with innumerable sins?" "Son," answered the father, encouraging him, "do not doubt: if you repent of them, in the name of God I promise you pardon." Then beginning to gain confidence, he said to the confessor: "Father, I believed myself lost, and despaired of salvation; but now I feel a sorrow for my sins, which encourages me to trust; and as God has not yet abandoned me, I wish to make my confession." And in fact on that day he made his confession

---

[57] L. 6, c. 97.

four times with great sorrow; the next day he received communion, and on the sixth he died, contrite and entirely resigned. After his death, Jesus Christ further revealed to St. Bridget, that this sinner was saved, and was in purgatory, and that he had been saved by the intercession of the Virgin, his mother; for the deceased, although he had led so sinful a life, yet had always preserved devotion to her dolors, whenever he remembered them, he pitied her.

PRAYER

Oh my afflicted mother! Queen of martyrs and of sorrows, thou hast shed so many tears for thy Son, who died for my salvation, and yet what will thy tears avail me, if I am lost? By the merits, then, of thy dolors, obtain for me a true sorrow for my sins, and a true amendment of life, with a perpetual and tender compassion for the passion of Jesus and thy own sufferings. And if Jesus and thou, being so innocent, have suffered so much for me, obtain for me that I, who am deserving of hell, may also suffer something for love of you. O Lady, I will say to thee with St. Bonaventure, if I have offended thee, wound my heart in punishment; if I have served thee, now I beg to be wounded as a reward. It is a shameful thing to see our Lord Jesus wounded, and thee wounded with him, and I uninjured.[58] Finally, oh my mother, by the grief thou didst experience on seeing thy Son before thy eyes bow his head and expire upon the cross, I entreat of thee to obtain for me a good death. Ah, do not cease, oh advocate of sinners, to assist my afflicted and struggling soul in that great passage that it has to make into eternity. And, because at that time it may easily be the case that I shall have lost the use of speech with which to invoke thy name, and that of Jesus, who are all my hope, therefore I now invoke thy

---

[58] O Domina, si te offendi pro justitia cor meum vulnera; si tibi servivi, nunc pro mercede, peto, vulnera. Opprobriosum est videre Dominum Jesum vulneratum, te convulneratum, et me illaesum.

Son and thee to succor me at that last moment, and I say: Jesus and Mary, to you I commend my soul. Amen.

ON THE FIRST DOLOR OF MARY

ST. SIMEON'S PROPHECY

In this valley of tears, every man is born to weep, and every one must suffer those afflictions that daily befall him. But how much more miserable would life be, if every one knew also the future evils which are to afflict him! Too unhappy would he be, says Seneca, whose fate was such.[1] The Lord exercises his compassion towards us, namely, that he does not make known to us the crosses that await us; that if we are to suffer them, at least we may suffer them only once. But he did not exercise this compassion with Mary, who, because God wished her to be the queen of dolors, and in all things like his Son, and to see always before her eyes, and to suffer continually all the sorrows that awaited her; and those were the sufferings of the passion and death of her beloved Jesus. For St. Simeon in the temple, after having received the divine child in his arms, predicted to her that this child was to be the mark for all the opposition and persecution of men; "Set for a sign which shall be contradicted;" and that

---

[1] Calamitosus esset animus futuri praescius et ante miserias miser. Ep. 98.

therefore the sword of sorrow should pierce her soul: "And thy own soul a sword shall pierce."[2]

The holy Virgin herself said to St. Matilda that, at the announcement of St. Simeon, all her joy was changed into sorrow.[3] For, as it was revealed to St. Theresa, the blessed mother, although she knew before this that the life of her Son would be sacrificed for the salvation of the world, yet she then learned more particularly and distinctly the sufferings and cruel death that awaited her poor Son. She knew that he would be contradicted in all things. Contradicted in doctrine; for instead of being believed, he would be esteemed a blasphemer for teaching that he was the Son of God, as the impious Caiaphas declared him to be, saying: "He hath blasphemed, he is guilty of death."[4] Contradicted in his reputation, for he was noble, of royal lineage, and was despised as a peasant: "Is not this the carpenter's son?"[5] "Is not this the carpenter, the son of Mary?"[6] He was wisdom itself, and was treated as an ignorant man: "How doth this man know letters, having never learned?"[7] As a false prophet: "And they blindfolded him and smote his face ... saying: Prophesy who is this that struck thee."[8] He was treated as a madman: "He is mad, why hear you him?"[9] As a wine-bibber, a glutton, and a friend of sinners: "Behold a man that is a glutton, and a drinker of wine, a friend of publicans and sinners."[10] As a sorcerer: "By the prince of devils he casteth out devils."[11] As a heretic and possessed person: "Do we not

---

[2] Positus est hic in signum cui contradicetur. Et tuam ipsius animam doloris gladius pertransibit. Luc. ii. 35.

[3] Omnis laetitia mea ad illa verba in moerore conversa est.

[4] Blasphemavit, reus est mortis. Matt. xxvi. 65, 66.

[5] Non hic fabri filius? Matt xiii. 55.

[6] Nonne hic est faber, filius Mariae? Matt. vi. 3.

[7] Quomodo hic literas scit, cum non didicerit. Joan. vii. 15.

[8] Et velaverunt eum, et percutiebant faciem ejus .... dicentes; Prophetiza, quis est qui te percussit. Luc. xxii. 64.

[9] Insanit, quid eum auditis? Joan. x. 20.

[10] Ecce homo devorator, et bibens vinum, amicus publicanorum et peccatorum. Luc. vii. 34.

[11] In principe daemoniorum ejicit daemonia. Matt. ix. 34.

say well of thee, that thou art a Samaritan, and hast a devil?"[12] In a word, Jesus was considered as so bad and notorious a man, that no trial was necessary to condemn him, as the Jews said to Pilate: "If he were not a malefactor, we would not have delivered him up to thee."[13] He was contradicted in his soul, for even his eternal Father, in order to give place to the divine justice, contradicted him by not wishing to hear him when he prayed to him, saying: "Father, if it be possible, let this chalice pass from me;"[14] and abandoned him to fear, weariness, and sadness, so that our afflicted Lord said: "My soul is sorrowful even unto death."[15] His interior suffering even caused him to sweat blood. Contradicted and persecuted, in a word, in his body and in his life, for he was tortured in all his sacred members: in his hands, in his feet, in his face, and in his head, in his whole body, till, drained to the last drop of his blood, he died an ignominious death on the cross.

When David, in the midst of all his pleasures and royal grandeur heard from Nathan the prophet, that his son should die – "The child that is born to thee shall surely die"[16] – he could find no peace, but wept, fasted, and slept upon the ground. Mary received with the greatest calmness the announcement that her Son should die, and peacefully continued to submit to it; but what grief she must have continually suffered, seeing this amiable Son always near her, hearing from him words of eternal life and beholding his holy demeanor. Abraham suffered great affliction during the three days he passed with his beloved Isaac, after he knew that he was to lose him. Oh God! not for three days, but for thirty-three years, Mary had to endure a like sorrow. *Like*, do I say? A sorrow as much greater as the Son of Mary was more lovely than the son of Abraham. The blessed Virgin herself

---

[12] Nonne bene dicimus nos, quia Samaritanus es tu, et daemonium habes? Joan.viii. 48.

[13] Si non esset hic malefactor, non tibi tradidissemus eum. Joan, xviii. 30.

[14] Pater mi, si possibile est, transeat a me calix iste. Matt, xxvi. 39

[15] Tristis es anima mea usque ad mortem. Matt. xxvi. 38.

[16] Filius qui natus est tibi, morte morietur. 2 Reg. xii. 14.

revealed to St. Bridget,[17] that while she lived on the earth there was not an hour when this grief did not pierce her soul: As often, she continued, as I looked upon my Son, as often as I wrapped him in his swaddling clothes, as often as I saw his hands and his feet, so often was my soul overwhelmed as it were with a fresh sorrow, because I considered how he would be crucified.[18] Rupert the Abbot, contemplating Mary, while she was suckling her Son, imagines her addressing him in these words: "'A bundle of myrrh is my beloved to me, he shall abide between my breasts.'[19] Ah, my Son, I clasp thee in my arms, because thou art so dear to me; but the dearer thou art to me, the more thou dost become to me a bundle of myrrh and of sorrow, when I think of thy sufferings." Mary, says St. Bernardine of Sienna,[20] considered that the strength of the saints was to pass through death; the beauty of paradise to be deformed; the Lord of the universe to be bound as a criminal; the Creator of all things to be livid with stripes; the Judge of all to be condemned; the glory of heaven despised; the King of kings to be crowned with thorns, and treated as a mock king.

Father Engelgrave writes that it was revealed to the same St. Bridget that the afflicted mother, knowing all that her Son would have to suffer, suckling him, thought of the gall and vinegar; when she swathed him, of the cords with which he was to be bound; when she bore him in her arms, she thought of him being nailed to the cross; and when he slept, she thought of his death.[21] As often as she put on him his clothes, she reflected that they would one day be torn

---

[17] Lib. 6, Rev. c. 9.

[18] Quoties aspiciebam filium meum, quoties involvebam eum pannis, quoties videbam ejus manus et pedes; toties animus meus quasi novo dolore absorptus est; quia cogitabam, quomodo crucifigeretur. Lib. 6, c. 57.

[19] Fasciculus mirrhae dilectus meus mihi, inter ubera mea commorabitur. Cant. i. 12.

[20] Tom. 3, Serm. 2, a 3, c. 1.

[21] Eum lactans cogitabat de felle et aceto; quando fasciis involvebat, funes cogitabat quibus ligandus erat; quando gestabat, cogitabat in cruce confixum; quando dormiebat, cogitabat mortuum. Tom. 1, Ev. Lu. Dom. infr. Oct. Nat. s. 1.

from him, that he might be crucified; and when she beheld his sacred hands and feet, and thought of the nails that were to pierce them, as Mary said to St. Bridget: "My eyes filled with tears, and my heart was tortured with grief."[22]

The evangelist says, that as Jesus Christ advanced in years, so also he advanced in wisdom and in grace with God and men.[23] That is, he advanced in wisdom and in grace before men or in their estimation; and before God, according to St. Thomas,[24] inasmuch as all his works would continually have availed to increase his merit, if from the beginning grace in its complete fulness had not been conferred on him by virtue of the hypostatic union. But if Jesus advanced in the esteem and love of others, how much more did he advance in Mary's love! But, oh God, as love increased in her, the more increased in her the grief of having to lose him by a death so cruel. And the nearer the time of the passion of her Son approached, with so much greater pain did that sword of sorrow, predicted by St. Simeon, pierce the heart of the mother; precisely this the angel revealed to St. Bridget, saying: "That sword of sorrow was every hour drawing nearer to the Virgin as the time for the passion of her Son drew nearer."[25]

If, then, Jesus our King and his most holy mother did not refuse, for love of us, to suffer during their whole life such cruel pains, there is no reason that we should complain if we suffer a little. Jesus crucified once appeared to Sister Magdalene Orsini, a Dominican nun, when she had been long suffering a great trial, and encouraged her to remain with him on the cross with that sorrow that was afflicting her. Sister Magdalene answered him complainingly: "Oh Lord, thou didst suffer on the cross only three hours, but it is more

---

[22] Oculi mei replebantur lacrymis, et cor meum torquebatur dolore. Lib. 6, c. 57. et 1. 7, c. 7.

[23] Et Jesus proficiebat sapientia et aetate, et gratia apud Deum, et homines. Luc. ii. 23.

[24] 3, p. q. 7, art. 12

[25] Ille doloris gladius Virgin! omni hora tanto se propius approximabat, quanto Filius passionis tempori magis appropinquabat. Fer. 6, lect. 2, c. 16.

than three years that I have been suffering this cross." Then the Redeemer replied: "Ah! ignorant soul, what dost thou say? I, from the first moment I was conceived, suffered in heart what I afterwards suffered on the cross." If, then, we too suffer any affliction and complain, let us imagine that Jesus and his mother Mary are saying to us the same words.

EXAMPLE

Father Roviglione, of the Company of Jesus, relates,[26] that a certain youth practised the devotion of visiting every day an image of the sorrowful Mary, in which she was represented with seven swords piercing her heart. One night the unhappy youth fell into mortal sin. Going next morning to visit the image, he saw in the heart of the blessed Virgin not only seven, but eight swords. As he stood gazing at this, he heard a voice saying to him that this sin had added the eighth sword to the heart of Mary. This softened his hard heart; he went immediately to confession, and through the intercession of his advocate, recovered the divine grace.

PRAYER

Oh, my blessed mother, not one sword only, but as many swords as I have committed sins have I added to those seven in thy heart. Ah, my Lady, thy sorrows are not due to thee who art innocent, but to me who am guilty. But since thou hast wished to suffer so much for me, ah, by thy merits obtain for me great sorrow for my sins, and patience under the trials of this life, which will always be light in comparison with my demerits, for I have often merited hell. Amen.

---

[26] Fase. di Rose, p. 2, c. 2

ON THE SECOND DOLOR OF MARY

THE FLIGHT OF JESUS INTO EGYPT

As the stag, wounded by an arrow, carries the pain with him wherever he goes, because he carries with him the arrow that has wounded him, thus the divine mother, after the prophecy of St. Simeon, as we saw in our consideration of the first grief, always carried her sorrow with her by the continual remembrance of the passion of her Son. Ailgrin, explaining this passage of the Canticles, "The hairs of thy head as the purple of the king bound in the channel,"[1] says: These hairs of Mary were her continual thoughts of the passion of Jesus, which kept always before her eyes the blood which was one day to flow from his wounds. Thy mind, oh Mary, and thy thoughts, tinged in the blood of the passion of our Lord, were always moved with sorrow as if they actually saw the blood flowing from his wounds.[2] Thus her Son

---

[1] Et comae capitis tui sicut purpura regis vincta canalibus. C. 7, v. 5

[2] Mens tua, O Maria, et cogitationes tuae tinctae in sanguine dorminicae passionis, sic affectae semper fuere, quasi recenter viderent sanguinem de vulneribus profluentem. In Cant. c. 7, v. 5.

himself was that arrow in the heart of Mary, who, the more worthy of love he showed himself to her, always wounded her the more with the sorrowful thought that she should lose him by so cruel a death. Let us now pass to the consideration of the second sword of sorrow which wounded Mary, in the flight of her infant Jesus into Egypt from the persecution of Herod.

Herod having heard that the expected Messiah was born, foolishly feared that the new-born King would deprive him of his kingdom. Hence St. Fulgentius, reproving him for his folly, thus says: "Why, oh Herod, art thou that disturbed? This King who is born has not come to conquer kings by arms, but to subjugate them, in a wonderful manner, by his death."[3] The impious Herod, therefore, waited to learn from the holy magi where the King was born, that he might take from him his life; but finding himself deceived by the magi, he ordered all the infants that could be found in the neighborhood of Bethlehem to be put to death. But an angel appeared in a dream to St. Joseph, and said to him: "Arise, and take the child and his mother, and fly into Egypt."[4] According to Gerson, immediately, on that very night, Joseph made this command known to Mary; and taking the infant Jesus, they commenced their journey, as it seems clearly from the Gospel itself: "Who arose and took the child and his mother by night, and retired into Egypt." Oh God, as blessed Albertus Magnus says in the name of Mary, must he, then, who came to save men flee from men? "Debet fugere qui salvator est mundi?"[5] And then the afflicted Mary knew that already the prophecy of Simeon, regarding her Son, was beginning to be verified – "He is set for a sign which shall be contradicted"[6] – seeing that scarcely is he born when he is persecuted to death. What

---

[3] Quid est quod sic turbaris Herodes? Rex iste qui natus est non venit reges pugnando superare sed moriendo mirabiliter subjugare. Serm. 5, de Epiph.

[4] Surge et accipe puerum, et matrem ejus et fuge in Egyptum. Matth. ii. 13.

[5] Qui consurgens accepit puerum et matrem ejus nocte, et secessit in Egyptum. Matth. ii. 14.

[6] Positus est hic in signum cui contradicetur.

suffering it must have been to the heart of Mary, writes St. John Chrysostom, to hear the tidings of that cruel exile of herself with her Son! Flee from thy friends to strangers, from the holy temple of the only true God to the temples of demons. What greater tribulation than that a new-born child, clinging to its mother's bosom, should be forced to fly with the mother herself![7]

Every one can imagine how much Mary must have suffered on this journey. It was a long distance to Egypt. Authors generally agree with Barrada[8] that it was four hundred miles; so that at least it was a journey of thirty days. The way, as St. Bonaventure describes it, was rough, unknown, through woods, and little frequented.[9] The season was winter, and therefore they had to travel in snow, rain, wind, and storms, and through bad and difficult roads. Mary was then fifteen years of age, a delicate virgin, unaccustomed to such journeys. They had no servant to attend them. Joseph and Mary, said St. Peter Chrysologus, had no man-servant nor maid-servant; they were themselves both masters and servants.[10] Oh God, how piteous a spectacle it was to see that tender Virgin, with that newly born infant in her arms wandering through this world! St. Bonaventure asks, Where did they obtain food? Where did they rest at night? How were they lodged?[11] What other food could they have, than a piece of hard bread which Joseph brought with him or begged in charity? Where could they have slept (particularly in the two hundred miles of desert through which they travelled, where, as authors relate, there were neither houses nor inns) except on the sand, or under some tree in the wood, in the open air, exposed to robbers, or those wild beasts with which

---

[7] Fuge a tuis ad extraneos, a templo ad daemonum fans. Quae major tribulatio, quam quod recens natus a collo matris pendens eum ipsa matre paupercula fugere cogatur?

[8] 3, Lib. 10, c. 8.

[9] Viam silvestrem, obscuram, asperam, et inhabitam.

[10] Joseph et Maria non habent famulum, non ancillam; ipsi domini et famuli.

[11] Quomodo faciebant de victu? Ubi nocte quiescebant? Quomodo hospitabantur. De Vit, Chr.

Egypt abounded? Ah, if any one had met these three greatest personages of the world, what would he have believed them to be but three poor, roving beggars?

They lived in Egypt, according to Brocard and Jansenius, in a district called Matures, though, according to St. Anselm, they dwelt in Heliopolis, first called Memphis, and now Cairo. And here let us consider the great poverty they must have suffered for the seven years they were there, as St. Antoninus, St. Thomas, and others assert. They were foreigners, unknown, without revenues, without money, without kindred; hardly were they able to support themselves by their humble labors. As they were destitute, says St. Basil, it is manifest what effort they must have made to obtain there the necessaries of life.[12] Moreover, Landolph of Saxony has written, and let it be repeated for the consolation of the poor, that so great was the poverty of Mary there, that sometimes she had not so much as a morsel of bread, when her Son, forced by hunger, asked it of her.[13]

St. Matthew also relates that when Herod was dead, the angel again appeared, in a dream, to St. Joseph, and directed him to return to Judea. St. Bonaventure, speaking of his return, considers the greater pain of the blessed Virgin, on account of the sufferings which Jesus must have endured in that journey, having arrived at about the age of seven years – an age, says the saint, when he was so large that he could not be carried, and so small that he could not go without assistance.[14]

The sight, then, of Jesus and Mary wandering like fugitives through this world, teaches us that we should also live as pilgrims on the earth, detached from the goods which the world offers us, as having soon to leave them and go to eternity. "We have not here a lasting city, but seek one that

---

[12] Cum enim essent egeni, manifestam est qnod sudores freqnentabant necesearia vitae inde sibi quaerentes.

[13] Aliquando filius famem patiens panem petit, nec unde dare mater habuit. In Vit. Christi. c. 13.

[14] Sic magnus est, at portari non valeat; et sic parvus quod per se ire non potest.

is to come."[15] To which St. Augustine adds: Thou art a stranger, thou givest a look, and then passest on: "Hospes es, vides et transis." It also teaches us to embrace crosses, for we cannot live in this world without a cross. The blessed Veronica da Binasco, an Augustinian nun, was carried in spirit to accompany Mary and the infant Jesus in this journey to Egypt, and at the end of it the divine mother said to her: "Child, hast thou seen through what difficulties we have reached this place? Now learn that no one receives graces without suffering." He who wishes to feel least the sufferings of this life, must take Jesus and Mary with him: "Accipe puerum et matrem ejus." For him who lovingly bears in his heart this Son and this mother, all sufferings become light, and even sweet and dear. Let us then love them, let us console Mary by receiving her Son within our hearts, whom, even now, men continue to persecute with their sins.

EXAMPLE

One day the most holy Mary appeared to the blessed Colletta, a Franciscan nun, and showed her the infant Jesus in a basin, torn in pieces, and then said to her: "Thus sinners continually treat my Son, renewing his death and my sorrows; oh, my daughter, pray for them that they may be converted."[16] Similar to this is that other vision which appeared to the venerable sister Jane, of Jesus and Mary, also a Franciscan nun. As she was one day meditating on the infant Jesus, persecuted by Herod, she heard a great noise, as of armed people, who were pursuing some one; and then appeared before her a most beautiful child, who was fleeing in great distress, and cried to her: "My Jane, help me, hide me; I am Jesus of Nazareth, I am flying from sinners who wish to kill me, and who persecute me as Herod did: do thou save me."[17]

---

[15] Non habemus hic manentem civitatem, sed futuram inquirimus. Heb. xiii. 14.
[16] Ap. P. Genev. Serv. Dol. di Mar.
[17] Loc. cit.

PRAYER

Then, oh Mary, even after thy Son hath died by the hands of men who persecuted him unto death, have not these ungrateful men yet ceased from persecuting him with their sins, and continuing to afflict thee, oh mother of sorrows? And I also, oh God, have been one of these. Ah, my most sweet mother, obtain for me tears to weep for such ingratitude. And then, by the sufferings thou didst experience in the journey to Egypt, assist me in the journey that I am making to eternity, that at length I may go to unite with thee in loving my persecuted Saviour, in the country of the blessed. Amen.

ON THE THIRD DOLOR OF MARY

THE LOSS OF JESUS IN THE TEMPLE

St. James the Apostle has said that our perfection consists in the virtue of patience. "And patience hath a perfect work, that you may be perfect and entire, failing in nothing."[1] The Lord having then given us the Virgin Mary as an example of perfection, it was necessary that she should be laden with sorrows, that in her we might admire and imitate her heroic patience. The dolor that we are this day to consider is one of the greatest which our divine mother suffered during her life, namely, the loss of her Son in the temple. He who is born blind is little sensible of the pain of being deprived of the light of day; but to him who has once had sight and enjoyed the light, it is a great sorrow to find himself deprived of it by blindness. And thus it is with those unhappy souls who, being blinded by the mire of this earth, have but little knowledge of God, and therefore scarcely feel pain at not finding him. On the contrary, the man who, illuminated

---

[1] Patientia autem opus perfectum habet, ut sitis perfecti et integri, in nullo deficientes. Jac. i. 4.

with celestial light, has been made worthy to find by love the sweet presence of the highest good, oh God, how he mourns when he finds himself deprived of it!

From this we can judge how painful must have been to Mary, who was accustomed to enjoy constantly the sweet presence of Jesus, that third sword which wounded her, when she lost him in Jerusalem, and was separated from him for three days.

In the second chapter of St. Luke, we read that the blessed Virgin, being accustomed to visit the temple every year at the paschal season, with Joseph her spouse and Jesus, once went when he was about twelve years old, and Jesus remained in Jerusalem, though she was not aware of it for she thought he was in company with others. When she reached Nazareth, she inquired for her Son, and not finding him there, she returned immediately to Jerusalem to seek him, but did not succeed until after three days. Now let us imagine what distress that afflicted mother must have experienced in those three days in which she was searching everywhere for her Son, with the spouse in the Canticles: "Have you seen him whom my soul loveth?"[2] But she could hear no tidings of him. Oh, with how much greater tenderness must Mary, overcome with fatigue, and yet not having found her beloved Son, have repeated those words of Ruben, concerning his brother Joseph: The boy doth not appear, and whither shall I go? "Puer non comparet, et ego quo ibo?" My Jesus doth not appear, and I know not what to do that I may find him; but where shall I go without my treasure? Weeping continually, she repeated during these three days with David: "My tears have been my bread, day and night, whilst it is said to me daily, Where is thy God?"[3] Wherefore Pelbart with reason says, that during those nights the afflicted mother had no rest, but wept and prayed without ceasing to God, that he

---

[2] Num quem diligit anima mea vidistis? Cant. iii. 3.
[3] Fuerunt mihi lacrymae meae panes die ac nocte, dum dicitur mihi quotidie, ubi est Deus tuus? Psal. xli. 4.

would enable her to find her Son.[4] And, according to St. Bernard, often during that time did she repeat to her Son himself the words of the spouse: "Show me where thou feedest, where thou liest in the mid-day, lest I begin to wander."[5] My Son, tell me where thou art, that I may no longer wander, seeking thee in vain.

Some writers assert, and not without reason, that this dolor was not only one of the greatest, but that it was the greatest and most painful of all. For in the first place, Mary in her other dolors had Jesus with her; she suffered when St. Simeon uttered the prophecy in the temple; she suffered in the flight to Egypt, but always with Jesus; but in this dolor she suffered at a distance from Jesus, without knowing where he was: "And the light of my eyes itself is not with me."[6] Thus, with tears, she then exclaimed: Ah, the light of my eyes, my dear Jesus, is no more with me; he is far from me, I know not where he is! Origen says that, though the love which this holy mother bore her Son, she suffered more at this loss of Jesus than any martyr ever suffered at death.[7] Ah, how long were these three days for Mary! – they appeared three ages. Very bitter days, for there was none to comfort her. And who, she exclaimed with Jeremias, who can console me if he who could console me is far from me? …and therefore my eyes are not satisfied with weeping: "Therefore do I weep, and my eyes run down with water, because the comforter is far from me."[8] And with Tobias she repeated: "What manner of joy shall be to me who sit in darkness, and see not the light of heaven?"[9]

---

[4] Illas noctes insomnes duxit in lacrymis, Deum deprecando, ut daret illi reperire filium.

[5] Indica, mihi ubi cubes, ubi pascas in meridie, ne vagari incipiam. Cant. i. 6.

[6] Lumen oculorum meorum, et ipse non est mecum. Psal. xxvii. 11.

[7] Vehementer doluit, quia vehementer amabat. Plus doluit de ejus amissione, quam aliquis martyr dolorem sentiat de animae a corpore separatione. Hom. infr. Oct. Ep.

[8] Idcirco ego plorans, et oculus meus deducens aquas, quia longe est a me consolator meus. Thren. i. 16.

[9] Quale gaudium erit mini, qui in tenebris sedeo, et lumen coeli non video. Tob. vi. 11.

Secondly – Mary understood well the cause and end of the other dolors, namely, the redemption of the world, the divine will; but in this she did not know the cause of the absence of her Son. The sorrowful mother was grieved to find Jesus withdrawn from her, for her humility, says Lanspergius, made her consider herself unworthy to remain with him any longer, and attend upon him on earth, and have the care of such a treasure.[10] And perhaps, she may have thought within herself, "I have not served him as I ought. Perhaps I have been guilty of some neglect, and therefore he has left me." They sought him, lest he perchance had left them, as Origen has said.[11] Certainly there is no greater grief for a soul that loves God than the fear of having displeased him. And therefore Mary never complained in any other sorrow but this, lovingly expostulating with Jesus after she found him: "Son, why hast thou done so to us? Thy father and I have sought thee sorrowing."[12] By these words she did not wish to reprove Jesus, as the heretics blasphemously assert, but only to make known to him the grief she had experienced during his absence from her, on account of the love she bore him. It was not a rebuke, says blessed Denis the Carthusian, but a loving complaint: "Non erat increpatio, sed amorosa conquestio." Finally, this sword so cruelly pierced the heart of the Virgin, that the blessed Benvenuta, desiring one day to share the pain of the holy mother in this dolor, and praying her to obtain for her this grace, Mary appeared to her with the infant Jesus in her arms; but while Benvenuta was enjoying the sight of that most beautiful child, in one moment she was deprived of it. So great was her sorrow that she had recourse to Mary, to implore her pity that it should not make her die of grief. The holy Virgin appeared to her again three days after, and said to her: "Now learn, oh my daughter, that

---

[10] Tristabatur ex humilitate, quia arbitrabatur se indignam cui tam pretiosus commissus esset thesaurus.

[11] Quaerebant eum, ne forte reliquisset eos. Ap. Corn, a Lap. in Luc. 2.

[12] Fili, quid fecisti nobis sic? Pater tuus et ego dolentes quaerebamus te. Luc. ii. 48.

thy sorrow is but a small part of that which I suffered when I lost my Son."[13]

This sorrow of Mary ought, in the first place, to serve as a comfort to those souls who are desolate and do not enjoy the sweet presence they once enjoyed of their Lord. They may weep, but let them weep in peace, as Mary wept in the absence of her Son. Let them take courage, and not fear that on this account they have lost the divine favor, for God himself said to St. Theresa: "No one is lost without knowing it; and no one is deceived without wishing to be deceived." If the Lord departs from the sight of that soul who loves him, he does not therefore depart from the heart. He often hides himself that she may seek him with greater desire and love. But those who would find Jesus must seek him, not amid the delights and pleasures of the world, but amid crosses and mortifications, as Mary sought him: We sought thee sorrowing, as she said to her Son: "Dolentes quaerebamus te." Learn from Mary to seek Jesus, says Origen: "Disce a Maria quaerere Jesum."

Moreover, in this world we should seek no other good than Jesus. Job was not unhappy when he lost all that he possessed on earth; riches, children, health, and honors, and even descended from a throne to a dunghill; but because he had God with him, even then he was happy. St. Augustine, speaking of him, says: He had lost all that God had given him, but he had God himself: "Perdiderat illa quae dederat Deus, sed habebat ipsum Deum." Unhappy and truly wretched are those souls who have lost God. If Mary wept for the absence of her Son for three days, how ought sinners to weep who have lost divine grace, to whom God says: "You are not my people, and I will not be yours."[14] For sin does this, namely, it separates the soul from God: "Your iniquities have divided between you and your God."[15] Hence, if even sinners possess all the goods of earth and have lost God, everything on earth

---

[13] March. Diar. 30, Ott.

[14] Vos non populus meus, et ego non ero vester. Os. i. 19.

[15] Peccata vestra diviserunt inter vos et Deum vestrum. Isa. lxix. 2.

becomes vanity and affliction to them, as Solomon confessed: "Behold, all is vanity and vexation of spirit."[16] But as St. Augustine says: The greatest misfortune of these poor blind souls is that, if they lose an ox, they do not fail to go in search of it; if they lose a sheep, they use all diligence to find it; if they lose a beast of burden, they cannot rest; but they lose the highest good, which is God, and yet they eat and drink, and take their rest.[17]

EXAMPLE

We read in the Annual Letters of the Society of Jesus, that in India, a young man who was just leaving his apartment in order to commit sin, heard a voice saying: "Stop, where are you going?" He turned round and saw an image, in relief, of the sorrowful Mary, who drew out the sword which was in her breast and said to him: "Take this dagger and pierce my heart rather than wound my Son with this sin." At the sound of these words the youth prostrated himself on the ground, and with deep contrition, bursting into tears, he asked and obtained from God and the Virgin pardon of his sin.

PRAYER

Oh, blessed Virgin, why art thou afflicted, seeking thy lost Son? Is it because thou dost not know where he is? But dost thou not know that he is in thy heart? Dost thou not see that he is feeding among the lilies? Thou thyself hast said it: "My beloved to me and I to him who feedeth among the lilies."[18] These, thy humble, pure, and holy thoughts and affections, are all lilies, that invite the divine spouse to dwell with thee. Ah, Mary, dost thou sigh after Jesus, thou who

---

[16] Ecce universa vanitas, et afflictio spiritus. Eccli. i. 14.
[17] Perdit homo bovem, et post eum vadit: perdit ovem et sollicite eam quaerit; perdit asinum, et non quiescit. Perdit homo Deum, et comedit, et bibit, et quiescit.
[18] Dilectus meus mihi, et ego illi, qui pascitur inter lilia. Cant. ii.16.

lovest none but Jesus? Leave sighing to me and so many other sinners who do not love him, and who have lost him by offending him. My most amiable mother, if through my fault thy Son hast not yet returned to my soul, wilt thou obtain for me that I may find him. I know well that he allows himself to be found by all who seek him: The Lord is good to the soul that seeketh him: "Bonus est Dominus ... animae quaerenti illum."[19] Make me to seek him as I ought to seek him. Thou art the gate through which all find Jesus; through thee I too hope to find him.

---

[19] Thren. iii. 25.

ON THE FOURTH DOLOR OF MARY

THE MEETING OF MARY WITH JESUS, WHEN HE WENT TO DEATH

St. Bernardine says that, to form an idea of the grief of Mary in losing her Jesus by death, it is necessary to consider the love that this mother bore to this her Son. All mothers feel the sufferings of their children as their own. Hence the woman of Chanaan, when she prayed the Saviour to deliver her daughter from the devil that tormented her, said to him, that he should have pity on the mother rather than on the daughter: "Have mercy on me, oh Lord, thou son of David, my daughter is grievously troubled by a devil."[1] But what mother ever loved a child so much as Mary loved Jesus? He was her only child, reared amidst so many troubles and pains; a most amiable child, and most loving to his mother; a Son, who was at the same time her Son and her God; who came on earth to kindle in the hearts of all the holy fire of divine love, as he himself declared: "I am come to cast fire on the earth,

---

[1] Miserere mei, Domine fili David, filia mea male a daemone vexatur. Matth. xv. 22.

and what will I but that it be kindled?"[2] Let us consider how he must have inflamed that pure heart of his holy mother, so free from every earthly affection. In a word, the blessed Virgin herself said to St. Bridget, that through love her heart and the heart of her Son were one: "Unum erat cor meum, et cor filii mei." That blending of handmaid and mother, of Son and God, kindled in the heart of Mary a fire composed of a thousand flames. But afterwards, at the time of the passion, this flame of love was changed into a sea of sorrow. Hence St. Bernardine says: All the sorrows of the world united would not be equal to the sorrow of the glorious Mary.[3] Yes, because this mother, as St. Lawrence Justinian writes: The more tenderly she loved, was the more deeply wounded.[4] The greater the tenderness with which she loved him, the greater was her grief at the sight of his sufferings, especially when she met her Son, after he had already been condemned, going to death at the place of punishment, bearing the cross. And this is the fourth sword of sorrow which today we have to consider.

The blessed Virgin revealed to St. Bridget that at the time when the passion of our Lord was drawing nigh, her eyes were always filled with tears, as she thought of her beloved Son whom she was about to lose on this earth. Therefore, as she also said, a cold sweat covered her body from the fear that seized her at that prospect of approaching suffering.[5] Behold, the appointed day at length arrived, and Jesus came in tears to take leave of his mother before he went to death. St. Bonaventure, contemplating Mary on that night, says: Thou didst spend it without sleep, and while others slept, thou didst remain watching.[6] Morning having arrived the disciples of Jesus Christ came to this afflicted mother, one,

---

[2] Ignem veni mittere in terram, et quid volo, nisi ut accendatur. Luc. xii. 49.

[3] Omnes dolores mundi, si essent simul conjuncti, non essent tanti quantus dolor gloriosae Mariae. Tom. iii. 5, 45.

[4] Quanto dilexit tenerius. tanto est vulnerata profundius.

[5] Imminente passione filii mei, lacrymae erant in oculis meis, et sudor in corpore prae timore. L. 1, Rev. c. 10.

[6] Sine somno duxisti, et soporatis caeteris, vigil permansisti.

to bring her this tidings, another, that; but all tidings of sorrow, for in her were then verified the words of Jeremias: "Weeping, she hath wept in the night, and her tears are on her cheeks; there is none to comfort her of all them that were dear to her."[7] One came to relate to her the cruel treatment of her Son in the house of Caiphas; another, the insults received by him from Herod. Finally, for I omit the rest to come to my point, St. John came and announced to Mary that the most unjust Pilate had already condemned him to death upon the cross. I say the most unjust, for, as St. Leo remarks, this unjust judge condemned him to death with the same lips with which he had pronounced him innocent.[8] Ah, sorrowful mother; said St. John to her, thy Son has already been condemned to death, he is already on his way, bearing himself his cross on his way to Calvary, as he afterwards related in his Gospel: "And bearing his own cross he went forth to that place which is called Calvary."[9] Come, if thou dost desire to see him and bid him a last farewell in some of the streets through which he is to pass.

Mary goes with St. John, and she perceives by the blood with which the way was sprinkled, that her Son had already passed there. This she revealed to St. Bridget: "By the footsteps of my Son I traced his course, for along the way by which he had passed, the ground was sprinkled with blood."[10] St. Bonaventure imagines the afflicted mother taking a shorter way, placing herself at the corner of the street to meet her afflicted Son as he passed by.[11] This most afflicted mother met her most afflicted Son: Moestissima mater moestissimo filio occurrit, said St. Bernard. While Mary stopped in that place, how much she must have heard said against her Son by the Jews who knew her, and perhaps also words in mockery

---

[7] Plorans ploravit in nocte, et lacrymse in maxillis ejus; non est qui consoletur eam, ex omnibus charis ejus. Thren. L 12.

[8] Iisdem labiis mittit ad mortem quibus eum pronuntiaverunt innocentem.

[9] Et bajulanis sibi crucem exivit in eum qui dicitur Calvariae locum. Joan. xix. 17.

[10] Ex vestigiis filii mei cognoscebam incessum ejus; quae enim procedenat, apparebat terra infusa sanguine. L. 4, c. 77.

[11] Med. 6

of herself! Alas! what a commencement of sorrows was then before her eyes, when she saw the nails, the hammers, the cords, the fatal instruments of the death of her Son borne before him! And what a sword pierced her heart when she heard the trumpet proclaiming along the way the sentence pronounced against her Son! But behold, now, after the instruments, the trumpet, and the ministers of justice had passed, she raises her eyes and sees; she sees, oh God, a young man covered with blood and wounds from head to foot, with a crown of thorns on his head, and two heavy beams on his shoulders; she looks at him and hardly knows him, saying, then, with Isaias: "And we have seen him, and there was no sightliness."[12] Yes, for the wounds, the bruises, and clotted blood, made him look like a leper; "We have thought him, as it were, a leper;"[13] so that he could no longer be recognized. "And his look was, as it were, hidden and despised, whereupon we esteemed him not."[14] But at length love recognizes him, and as soon as she knows him, ah, what was then, as St. Peter of Alcantara says in his meditations, the love and fear of the heart of Mary! On the one hand, she desired to see him; on the other, she could not endure to look upon so pitiable a sight. But at length they look at each other. The Son wipes from his eyes the clotted blood, which prevented him from seeing (as was revealed to St. Bridget), and looks upon the mother; the mother looks upon the Son. Ah, looks of sorrow, which pierced, as with so many arrows, those two holy and loving souls. When Margaret, the daughter of Sir Thomas More, met her father on his way to the scaffold, she could utter only two words, oh, father! oh, father! and fell fainting at his feet. At the sight of her Son going to Calvary, Mary fainted not; no, because it was not fitting that his mother should lose the use of her reason, as Father Suarez remarks, neither did she die, for God reserved

---

[12] Et vidimus eum, et non erat aspectus. Isa. liii. 2.
[13] Putavimus eum quasi leprosum. Isa. liii. 4.
[14] Et quasi absconditus vultus ejus, et despectus, unde nec reputavimus eum. Isa. liii. 3.

her for a greater grief; but if she did not die, she suffered sorrow enough to cause her a thousand deaths.

The mother wished to embrace him, as St. Anselm says, but the officers of justice thrust her aside, loading her with insults, and urge onward our afflicted Lord. Mary follows. Ah, holy Virgin, where art thou going? To Calvary! And canst thou trust thyself to see him who is thy life hanging from a cross? And thy life shall be as it were hanging before thee: "Et erit vita tua quasi pendens ante te."[15] Ah! my mother, stop, says St. Lawrence Justinian, as if the Son himself had then spoken to her; where dost thou hasten? Where art thou going? If thou comest where I go, thou wilt be tortured with my sufferings, and I with thine.[16] But although the sight of her dying Jesus must cost her such cruel anguish, the loving Mary will not leave him. The Son goes before, and the mother follows, that she may be crucified with her Son, as William the Abbot says: The mother took up her cross, and followed him, that she might be crucified with him.[17] We even pity the wild beasts: "Ferarum etiam miseremur," as St. John Chrysostom has said. If we should see a lioness following her whelp as he was led to death, even this wild beast would call forth our compassion. And shall we not feel compassion to see Mary following her immaculate Lamb, as they are leading him to death? Let us then pity her, and endeavor also ourselves to accompany her Son and herself, bearing with patience the cross which the Lord imposes upon us. Why did Jesus Christ, asks St. John Chrysostom, desire to be alone in his other sufferings, but in bearing the cross wished to be helped by the Cyrenean? And he answers: That thou mayest understand that the cross of Christ is not sufficient without thine.[18] The cross alone of Jesus is not enough to save us, if we do not bear with resignation also our own, even unto death.

---

[15] Deut. xxviii. 66.

[16] Heu quo properas, quo venis mater! Cruciatu meo cruciaberis et ego tuo.

[17] Tollebat et mater crucem suam, et sequebatur eum, crucifigenda sum ipso. In Cant. 7.

[18] Ut intelligas Christi crucem non sufficere sine tua.

EXAMPLE

The Saviour appeared one day to sister Diomira, a nun, in Florence, and said to her, "Think of me, and love me, and I will think of thee, and love thee," and at the same time he presented her with a bunch of flowers and a cross, signifying to her by this that the consolations of the saints on this earth are always to be accompanied by the cross. The cross unites souls to God. Blessed Jerome Emilian, when he was a soldier, and leading a very sinful life, was shut up by his enemies in a tower. There, feeling deeply his misfortune, and enlightened by God to amend his life, he had recourse to the most holy Mary, and then with the help of this divine mother, he began to live the life of a saint. By this he merited to see once in heaven the high place which God had prepared for him. He became founder of the order of Sommaschi, died a saint, and has been lately beatified by the holy Church.

PRAYER

My sorrowful mother, by the merit of that grief which thou didst feel at seeing thy beloved Jesus led to death, obtain for me the grace also to bear with patience those crosses which God sends me. Happy me, if I also shall know how to accompany thee with my cross until death. Thou and Jesus, both innocent, have borne a heavy cross; and shall I a sinner, who have merited hell, refuse mine? Ah, immaculate Virgin, I hope that thou wilt help me to bear my crosses with patience. Amen.

ON THE FIFTH DOLOR OF MARY

THE DEATH OF JESUS

And now we have to admire a new sort of martyrdom, a mother condemned to see an innocent son, whom she loved with all the affection of her heart, put to death before her eyes, by the most barbarous tortures. There stood by the cross of Jesus his mother: "Stabat autem juxta crucem mater ejus." There is nothing more to be said, says St. John, of the martyrdom of Mary: behold her at the foot of the cross, looking on her dying Son, and then see if there is grief like her grief. Let us stop then also today on Calvary, to consider this fifth sword that pierced the heart of Mary, namely, the death of Jesus.

As soon as our afflicted Redeemer had ascended the hill of Calvary, the executioners stripped him of his garments, and piercing his sacred hands and feet with nails, not sharp, but blunt: "Non acutis, sed obtusis," as St. Bernard says,[1] and to torture him more, they fastened him to the cross. When they had crucified him, they planted the cross, and thus left

---

[1] Serm, 2, de Pass.

him to die. The executioners abandon him, but Mary does not abandon him. She then draws nearer to the cross, in order to assist at his death. "I did not leave him," thus the blessed Virgin revealed to St. Bridget, "and stood nearer to his cross."[2] But what did it avail, oh Lady, says St. Bonaventure, to go to Calvary to witness there the death of this Son? Shame should have prevented thee, for his disgrace was also thine, because thou wast his mother; or, at least, the horror of such a crime, as that of seeing a God crucified by his own creatures, should have prevented thee.[3] But the saint himself answers: Thy heart did not consider the horror, but the suffering: "Non considerabat cor tuum horrorem, sed dolorem." Ah, thy heart did not then care for its own sorrow, but for the suffering and death of thy dear Son; and therefore thou thyself didst wish to be near him, at least to compassionate him. Ah, true mother! says William the Abbot, loving mother! for not even the terror of death could separate thee from thy beloved Son.[4] But, oh God, what a spectacle of sorrow, to see this Son then in agony upon the cross, and under the cross this mother in agony, who was suffering all the pain that her Son was suffering! Behold the words in which Mary revealed to St. Bridget the pitiable state of her dying Son, as she saw him on the cross: "My dear Jesus was on the cross in grief and in agony; his eyes were sunken, half closed, and lifeless; the lips hanging, and the mouth open; the cheeks hollow, and attached to the teeth; the face lengthened, the nose sharp, the countenance sad; the head had fallen upon his breast, the hair black with blood, the stomach collapsed, the arms and legs stiff, and the whole body covered with wounds and blood."[5]

Mary also suffered all these pains of Jesus. Every torture inflicted on the body of Jesus, says St. Jerome, was a wound

---

[2] Ego non separabar ab eo, et stabam vicinior cruci ejus. L. 1, c. 6.
[3] Cur ivisti, O Domina, ad Calvariae locum? cur te non retinuit pudor, horror facinoris?
[4] Plane mater, quae nec in terrore mortis filium deserebat. Serm. 8, de Ass.
[5] L. 1, Rev. c. 10, et 1. 4, c. 70.

in the heart of the mother.[6] Any one of us who should then have been on Mount Calvary, would have seen two altars, says St. John Chrysostom, on which two great sacrifices were consummating, one in the body of Jesus, the other in the heart of Mary. But rather would I see there, with St. Bonaventure, one altar only, namely, the cross alone of the Son, on which, with the victim, this divine Lamb, the mother also was sacrificed. Therefore the saint interrogates her in these words: Oh Lady, where art thou? Near the cross? Nay, on the cross, thou art crucified with thy Son.[7] St. Augustine also says the same thing: The cross and nails of the Son were also the cross and nails of the mother; Christ being crucified, the mother was also crucified.[8] Yes, because, as St. Bernard says, love inflicted on the heart of Mary the same suffering that the nails caused in the body of Jesus.[9] Therefore, at the same time that the Son was sacrificing his body, the mother, as St. Bernardine says, was sacrificing her soul.[10]

Mothers fly from the presence of their dying children; but if a mother is ever obliged to witness the death of a child, she procures for him all possible relief; she arranges the bed, that his posture may be more easy; she administers refreshments to him; and thus the poor mother relieves her own sorrows. Ah, mother, the most afflicted of all mothers! oh Mary, it was decreed that thou shouldst be present at the death of Jesus, but it was not given to thee to afford him any relief. Mary heard her Son say: I thirst: "Sitio;" but it was not permitted her to give him a little water to quench his great thirst. She could only say to him, as St. Vincent Ferrer remarks: My Son, I have only the water of my tears: "Fili, non habeo nisi aquara lacrymarum."[11] She saw that her Son,

---

[6] Quot laesiones in corpore Christi, tot vulnera in corde matris. Ap. Bald. to. 1, p. 499.
[7] O Domina, ubi stas? Numquid juxta crucem? Imo in cruce cum filio cruciaris? Ap. Bald. tom. 1, p. 452.
[8] Crux et clavi filii fuerunt et matris; Christo crucifixo crucifigebatur et mater.
[9] Quod in carne Christi agebant clavi, in Virginis mente affectus erga filium.
[10] Dum illi corpus, ista spiritum immolabat. To. 1, Serm. 31.
[11] Ap. Bald. p. 456.

suspended by three nails to that bed of sorrow, could find no rest. She wished to clasp him to her heart, that she might give him relief, or at least that he might expire in her arms, but she could not.[12] She only saw that poor Son in a sea of sorrow, seeking one who could console him as he had predicted by the mouth of the prophet: "I have trodden the winepress alone; I looked about and there was none to help; I sought and there was none to give aid."[13] But who was there among men to console him, if all were his enemies? Even on the cross they cursed and mocked him on every side: "And they that passed by blasphemed him, wagging their heads."[14] Some said to him: "If thou be the Son of God, come down from the cross."[15] Some exclaimed: "He saved others, himself he cannot save."[16] Others said: "If he be the King of Israel, let him come down from the cross."[17] The blessed Virgin herself said to St. Bridget: "I heard some call my Son a thief; I heard others call him an impostor; others said that no one deserved death more than he; and every word was to me a new sword of sorrow."[18]

But what increased most the sorrows which Mary suffered through compassion for her Son, was to hear him complain on the cross that even the eternal Father had abandoned him: "My God, my God, why hast thou forsaken me?"[19] Words which, as the divine mother herself said to St. Bridget, could never depart from her mind during her whole life.[20] Thus the afflicted mother saw her Jesus suffering on every side; she desired to comfort him, but could not. And what caused her the greatest sorrow was to see that, by her presence and her grief, she increased the sufferings of her

---

[12] Volebat eum amplecti sed manus frustra protersae in se complexae redibant Ap. Bald. 463.
[13] Torcular calcavi solus … Circumspexi, et non est auxiliator; quaesivi, et non fuit qui adjuvaret. Isa. lxiii. 3, 5.
[14] Praetereuntes autem blasphemabant eum moventes capita sua. Matt, xxvii. 39.
[15] Si filius Dei es, descende de cruce.
[16] Alios salvos fecit, seipsum non potest salvum facere.
[17] Si rex Israel est, descendat nunc de cruce. Loc. cit.
[18] Rev. 1. 4, c. 70.
[19] Deus, Deus meus, ut quid dereliquisti me? Matth. xxvii. 48.
[20] Rev. 1. 4, c. 70.

Son. The sorrow itself, says St. Bernard, that filled the heart of Mary, increased the bitterness of sorrow in the heart of Jesus.[21] St. Bernard also says that Jesus on the cross suffered more from compassion for his mother than from his own pains: he thus speaks in the name of the Virgin: I stood and looked upon him, and he looked upon me; and he suffered more for me than for himself.[22] The same saint also, speaking of Mary beside her dying Son, says that she lived dying without being able to die: Near the cross stood his mother, speechless; living she died, dying she lived; neither could she die, because she was dead, being yet alive.[23] Passino writes that Jesus Christ himself, speaking one day to the blessed Baptista Varana, of Camerino, said to her, that he was so afflicted on the cross at the sight of his mother in such anguish at his feet, that compassion for his mother caused him to die without consolation. So that the blessed Baptista, being enlightened to know this suffering of Jesus, exclaimed: Oh my Lord, tell me no more of this thy sorrow, for I cannot bear it.

Men were astonished, says Simon of Cassia, when they saw this mother then keep silence, without uttering a complaint in this great suffering.[24] But if the lips of Mary were silent, her heart was not so; for she did not cease offering to divine justice the life of her Son for our salvation. Therefore, we know that by the merits of her dolors she co-operated with Christ in bringing us forth to the life of grace, and therefore we are children of her sorrows: Christ, says Lanspergius, wished her whom he had appointed for our mother to co-operate with him in our redemption; for she herself at the foot of the cross was to bring us forth as her

---

[21] Repleta matre, ad filium redundaret inundatio amaritudims. Hom. in Ev. Stabat.

[22] Stabam ego videns eum, ipse videns me, et plus dolebat de me quam de se. Ap. Simisc. Cons. 28.

[23] Juxta crucem stabat mater, vox illi non erat; moriebatur vivens, vivebat moriens; nee mori poterat, quia vivens mortua erat. De. Lament. Virg.

[24] Stupebant omnes qui noverant hujus hominis matrem, quod etiam in tantae augustiae pressura silentium servabat.

children.[25] And if ever any consolation entered into that sea of bitterness, namely, the heart of Mary, it was this only one; namely, the knowledge that by means of her sorrows, she was bringing us to eternal salvation; as Jesus himself revealed to St. Bridget: "My mother Mary, on account of her compassion and charity, was made mother of all in heaven and on earth."[26] And, indeed, these were the last words with which Jesus took leave of her before his death; this was his last remembrance, leaving us to her for her children in the person of John, when he said to her: Woman,[27] behold thy Son: "Mulier ecce filius tuus."[28] And from that time Mary began to perform for us this office of a good mother; for, as St. Peter Damian declares, the penitent thief, through the prayers of Mary, was then converted and saved: Therefore the good thief repented, because the blessed Virgin, standing between the cross of her Son and that of the thief, prayed her Son for him; thus rewarding, by this favor, his former service.[29] For as other authors also relate, this thief, in the journey to Egypt with the infant Jesus, showed them kindness; and this same office the blessed Virgin has ever continued, and still continues to perform.

EXAMPLE

A young man in Perugia once promised the devil that if he would help him to commit a sinful act which he desired to do, he would give him his soul; and he gave him a writing to

---

[25] Voluit eam Christus cooperatricem nostrae redemptionis adstare, quam nobis constituerat dare matrem; debebat enim ipsa sub cruce nos parere filios. Hom. 44, de Pass. Dom.

[26] Maria mater mea, propter compassionem et charitatem facta est mater omnium in coelis et in terra. L. 1, c. 31.

[27] In a different edition of *The Glories of Mary*, St. Alphonsus added, "He called her *woman* that, by the sweet name of *Mother*, He might not increase her grief." -SDP

[28] Joan. xix. 26.

[29] Idcirco resipuit bonus latro, quia B. Virgo inter cruces filii et latronis posita, filium pro latrone deprecabatur; hoc suo beneficie, antiquum latronis obsequium recompensans. Ap. Salm. to. 1, tr. 47.

that effect, signed with his blood. The evil deed was committed, and the devil demanded the performance of the promise. He led the young man to a well, and threatened to take him body and soul to hell if he would not cast himself into it. The wretched youth, thinking that it would be impossible for him to escape from his enemy, climbed the well-side in order to cast himself into it, but terrified at the thought of death, he said to the devil that he had not the courage to throw himself in, and that, if he wished to see him dead, he himself should thrust him in. The young man wore about his neck the scapular of the sorrowing Mary; and the devil said to him: "Take off that scapular, and I will thrust you in." But the youth, seeing the protection which the divine mother still gave him through that scapular, refused to take it off, and after a great deal of altercation, the devil departed in confusion. The sinner repented, and grateful to his sorrowful mother, went to thank her, and presented a picture of this case, as an offering, at her altar in the new church of Santa Maria, in Perugia.[30]

PRAYER

Ah, mother, the most afflicted of all mothers, thy Son, then, is dead; thy Son so amiable, and who loved thee so much! Weep, for thou hast reason to weep. Who can ever console thee? Nothing can console thee but the thought that Jesus, by his death, hath conquered hell, hath opened paradise, which was closed to men, and hath gained so many souls. From that throne of the cross he was to reign over so many hearts, which, conquered by his love, would serve him with love. Do not disdain, oh my mother, to keep me near to weep with thee, for I have more reason than thou to weep for the offences that I have committed against thy Son. Ah, mother of mercy, I hope for pardon and my eternal salvation, first through the death of my Redeemer, and then through the merits of thy dolors. Amen.

---

[30] Monum. Conv. Pec. ap. P. Sinisch. Sans. 16.

ON THE SIXTH DOLOR OF MARY

THE PIERCING OF THE SIDE OF JESUS, AND HIS DESCENT FROM THE CROSS

"Oh, all ye that pass by the way attend, and see if there be any sorrow like to my sorrow."[1] Devout souls, listen to what the sorrowful Mary says to you today: My beloved children, I do not wish you to console me; no, for my heart can never again be consoled on this earth after the death of my dear Jesus. If you wish to please me, this I ask of you, turn to me and see if there has ever been in the world a grief like mine, when I saw him who was all my love torn from me so cruelly. But, oh Lady, since thou dost not wish to be consoled, and hast such a thirst for suffering, I must say to thee that thy sorrows have not ended with the death of thy Son. Today thou wilt be pierced by another sword of sorrow, when thou shalt see a cruel lance piercing the side of this thy Son, already dead, and shalt receive him in thy arms after he is taken from the cross. And now we are to consider today the sixth dolor which afflicted this sorrowful mother. Attend and

---

[1] O vos omnes qui transitis per viam, attendite et videte, si est dolor sicut dolor meus. Thren. i. 12.

weep. Hitherto the dolors of Mary tortured her one by one, but to-day they are all united to assail her.

To make known to a mother that her child is dead is sufficient to kindle her whole soul with love for the lost one. Some persons, in order to lighten their grief, will remind mothers whose children have died, of the displeasure they had once caused them. But if I, oh my queen, should wish to lighten thy sorrow for the death of Jesus in this way, what displeasure has he ever caused thee, that I could recall to thy mind? Ah, no; he always loved thee, obeyed thee, and respected thee. Now thou hast lost him, and who can describe thy sorrow? Do thou who hast felt it explain it. A devout author says, that when our Redeemer was dead, the heart of the great mother was first engaged in accompanying the most holy soul of the Son, and presenting it to the eternal Father. "I present thee, oh my God," Mary must then have said, "the immaculate soul of thy and my Son, which has been obedient to thee even unto death: receive it, then, in thy arms. Thy justice is now satisfied, thy will accomplished; behold, the great sacrifice to thy eternal glory is consummated." And then turning to the lifeless members of her Jesus: Oh wounds, she said, oh loving wounds, I adore you, I rejoice with you, since through you salvation has been given to the world. You shall remain open in the body of my Son, to be the refuge of those who will have recourse to you. Oh, how many, through you, shall receive the pardon of their sins, and then through you shall be inflamed to love the Sovereign Good!

That the joy of the following Paschal Sabbath should not be disturbed, the Jews wished the body of Jesus to be taken down from the cross; but because they could not take down a criminal until he was dead, they came with iron mallets to break his legs, as they had already done to the two thieves crucified with him. And Mary, while she remains weeping at the death of her Son, sees those armed men coming towards her Jesus. At this sight she first trembled with fear, then she said: Ah, my Son is already dead, cease to maltreat him, and cease to torture me a poor mother longer. She implored them not to break his legs: "Oravit eos, ne frangerent crura," as St. Bonaventure writes. But while she is thus speaking, oh, God! she sees a soldier with violence brandishing a spear, and piercing the side of Jesus: "One of the soldiers with a spear opened his side, and immediately there came out blood and water."[2] The cross shook at the stroke of the spear, and, as was revealed to St. Bridget, the heart of Jesus was divided: "Ita ut ambae paries essent divisae."[3] There came out blood and water, for only a few drops of blood remained, and those also the Saviour wished to shed, in order to show that he had no more blood to give us. The injury of that stroke was offered to Jesus, but the pain was inflicted on Mary: Christ, says the devout Lanspergius, shared with his mother the infliction of that wound, for he received the insult and his mother the pain.[4] The holy Fathers explain this to be the very sword predicted to the Virgin by St. Simeon; a sword, not of iron, but of grief, which pierced through her blessed soul in the heart of Jesus, where it always dwelt. Thus, among others, St. Bernard says: The spear which opened his side passed through the soul of the Virgin, which could not be torn from the heart of Jesus.[5] And the divine mother herself revealed the same to St. Bridget, saying: "When the spear was drawn out, the point appeared red with blood; then I felt as if my heart were pierced when I saw the heart of my most dear Son pierced."[6] The angel told St. Bridget, that such were the sufferings of Mary, that she was saved from death only by the miraculous power of God.[7] In her other dolors she at least

---

[2] Unus militum lancea latus ejus aperuit, et continuo exivit sanguis, et aqua. Joan. xix. 34.

[3] Rev. l. 2, c. 21.

[4] Divisit Christus cum matre sua hujus vulneris poenam, ut ipse injuriam acciperet, mater dolorem.

[5] Lancea quae ipsius latus aperuit, animam Virginis pertransivit, quae inde nequibat avelli. De Lament. Virg.

[6] Cum retraheretur hasta, apparuit cuspia rubea sanguine. Tunc mihi videbatur quod quasi cor meum perforaretur, cum vidissem cor filii mei charissimi perforatum. Rev. c. 10.

[7] Non parvum miraculum a Deo factum est, quod B. Virgo tot doloribus sauciata spiritum non exhalarit.

had her Son to compassionate her; and now she had not even him to take pity on her.

The afflicted mother, still fearing that other injuries might be inflicted on her Son, entreats Joseph of Arimathea to obtain from Pilate the body of her Jesus, that at least after his death she may be able to guard it and protect it from injuries. Joseph went to Pilate and made known to him the sorrow and the wish of this afflicted mother; and St. Anselm thinks that compassion for the mother softened the heart of Pilate, and moved him to grant her the body of the Saviour. And now Jesus is taken from the cross. Oh, most holy Virgin, after thou with so great love hadst given thy Son to the world for our salvation, behold the world returns him to thee again! "But oh, my God, how dost thou return him to me?" said Mary to the world. "My Son was white and ruddy: 'Dilectus meus candidus et rubicundus:' but thou hast returned him to me blackened with bruises, and red, not with a ruddy color, but with the wounds thou hast inflicted upon him; he was beautiful, now there is no more beauty in him; he is all deformity." All were enamored with his aspect, now he excites horror in all who look upon him. Oh, how many swords, says St. Bonaventure, pierced the soul of this mother, when she received the body of her Son after it was taken from the cross: "O quot gladii animam matris pertransierunt!" Let us consider what anguish it would cause any mother to receive the lifeless body of a son! It was revealed to St. Bridget that, to take down the body of Jesus, three ladders were placed against the cross. Those holy disciples first drew out the nails from the hands and feet, and according to Metaphrastes, gave them in charge to Mary. Then one supported the upper part of the body of Jesus, the other the lower, and thus took it down from the cross. Bernardine de Bustis describes the afflicted mother as raising herself and extending her arms to meet her dear Son; she embraces him, and then sits down at the foot of the cross. She sees his mouth open, his eyes shut; she examines the lacerated flesh, and those exposed bones; she takes off the crown, and sees the cruel injury made by those thorns in that sacred head; she looks upon those pierced hands and feet, and says: Ah, my Son, to what has the love thou didst bear to men reduced thee! But what evil hast thou done to them, that they have treated thee so cruelly? "Thou wast my Father," Bernardine de Bustis imagines her to say, "my brother, my spouse, my delight, my glory, my all."[8] Oh, my Son, behold how I am afflicted, look upon me and console me; but thou dost look upon me no more. Speak, speak to me but one word, and console me; but thou dost speak no more, for thou art dead. Then turning to those barbarous instruments, she said: Oh, cruel thorns, oh nails, oh merciless spear, how could you thus torture your Creator? But what thorns, what nails? Alas! sinners, she exclaimed, it is you who have thus cruelly treated my Son.

Thus Mary spoke and complained of us. But if now she were capable of suffering, what would she say? What grief would she feel to see that men after the death of her Son, continue to torment and crucify him by their sins? Let us no longer give pain to this sorrowful mother; and if we also have hitherto grieved her by our sins, let us now do what she directs. She says to us: Return, ye transgressors, to the heart: "Redite, praevaricatores, ad cor."[9] Sinners, return to the wounded heart of my Jesus; return as penitents, for he will receive you. Flee from him to him, she continues to say with Guerric the Abbot; from the Judge to the Redeemer, from the tribunal to the cross.[10] The Virgin herself revealed to St. Bridget that she closed the eyes of her Son, when he was taken down from the cross, but she could not close his arms: "Ejus brachia flectere non potui." Jesus Christ giving us to understand by this that he desired to remain with open arms to receive all penitent sinners who return to him. Oh world, continues Mary, behold, then, thy time is the time of lovers:

---

[8] Tu mihi pater eras, tu frater, sponsus, meae deliciae, mea gloria, tu mihi omnia eras.
[9] Isa. xlvi
[10] Ab ipso fnge ad ipsum, a judice ad redemptorem, a tribunali ad crucem.

"Et ecce, tempus tuum, tempus amantium."[11] Now that my Son, oh world, has died to save thee, this is no longer for thee a time of fear, but of love: a time to love him who has desired to suffer so much in order to show thee the love he bore thee. Therefore, says St. Bernard, is the heart of Jesus wounded that, through the visible wound, the invisible wound of love may be seen.[12] If then, concludes Mary, in the words of the Abbot of Celles, my Son had wished his side to be opened that he might give thee his heart,[13] it is right, oh man, that thou shouldst give him thy heart. And if you wish, oh children of Mary, to find a place in the heart of Jesus without fear of being cast out, go, says Ubertino of Casale, go with Mary, for she will obtain grace for you;[14] and in the following example we have a beautiful proof of this.

EXAMPLE

The Disciple relates[15] that there was once a poor sinner who, among other crimes, had killed his father and a brother, and therefore became a fugitive. Happening to hear, one day during Lent, a sermon upon the divine mercy, he went to the preacher himself to make his confession. The confessor having heard his crimes, sent him to an altar of the sorrowful mother to pray that she might obtain for him compunction and pardon of his sins. The sinner obeyed, and began to pray, when behold, suddenly overpowered by contrition, he falls down dead. On the following day when the priest recommended to the people to pray for the deceased, a white dove appeared in the church and let fall a card at the feet of the priest. He took it up, and found these words written on it: "The soul of the dead, when it left the body, immediately

---

[11] Ezech. xvi. 8
[12] Propterea vulneratum est cor Christi, ut per vulnus visibile vulnus amoris invisibilis videatur. Serm. de pass. Dom.
[13] Prae nimio amore aperuit sibi latus, ut praeberet cor suum.
[14] Filii hujus matris, ingredite um ipsa intra penetralia cordis Jesu
[15] Promt. Ex. V. Miser.

went to paradise; and do you continue to preach the infinite mercy of God."

PRAYER

Oh, afflicted Virgin! oh soul, great in virtues and great also in sorrows! for both arise from that great fire of love thou hast for God; thou "whose heart can love nothing but God; ah mother, have pity on me, for I have not loved God, and I have so much offended him. Thy sorrows give me great confidence to hope for pardon. But this is not enough; I wish to love my Lord, and who can better obtain this for me than thou – thou who art the mother of fair love? Ah Mary, thou dost console all, comfort me also. Amen.

ON THE SEVENTH DOLOR OF MARY

THE BURIAL OF THE BODY OF JESUS

When a mother is by the side of a suffering and dying child, she no doubt then feels and suffers all his pains; but when the afflicted child is really dead and about to be buried, and the sorrowful mother takes her last leave of him, oh God! the thought that she is to see him no more is a sorrow that exceeds all other sorrows. Behold, the last sword of sorrow which we are to consider, when Mary, after being present at the death of her Son upon the cross, after having embraced his lifeless body, was finally to leave him in the sepulchre, never more to enjoy his beloved presence.

But that we may better understand this last dolor, let us return to Calvary, again to look upon the afflicted mother, who still holds, clasped in her arms, the lifeless body of her Son. "Oh my Son," she seems then to continue to say in the words of Job, "my Son, thou art changed to be cruel towards me: 'Mutatus es mihi in crudelem.'[1] Yes, for all thy beauty, grace, virtue, and loveliness, all the signs of special love thou

---

[1] C. xxx. 21.

hast shown me, the peculiar favors thou hast bestowed on me, are all changed into so many darts of sorrow, which the more they have inflamed my love for thee, so much the more cause me cruelly to feel the pain of having lost thee. Ah, my beloved Son, in losing thee I have lost all." Thus St. Bernard speaks in her name: Oh truly begotten of God, thou wast to me a father, a son, a spouse; thou wast my life! Now I am deprived of my father, my spouse, and my Son, for with my Son whom I have lost, I lose all things.[2]

Thus Mary, clinging to her Son, was dissolved in grief; but those holy disciples, fearing lest this poor mother would expire there through agony, went to take the body of her Son from her arms, to bear it away for burial. Therefore, with reverential force they took him from her arms, and having embalmed him, wrapped him in a linen cloth already prepared, upon which our Lord wished to leave to the world his image impressed, as may be seen at the present day in Turin. And now they bear him to the sepulchre. The sorrowful funeral train sets forth; the disciples place him on their shoulders; hosts of angels from heaven accompany him; those holy women follow him; and the afflicted mother follows in their company her Son to the grave. When they had reached the appointed place, how gladly would Mary have buried herself there alive with her Son! "Oh how willingly," said the Virgin to St. Bridget, "would I have remained there alive with my Son, if it had been his will!"[3] But since this was not the divine will, the authors relate that she herself accompanied the sacred body of Jesus into the sepulchre, where, as Baronius narrates, they deposited the nails and the crown of thorns. In raising the stone to close the sepulchre, the disciples of the Saviour had to turn to the Virgin, and say to her: Now, oh Lady, we must close the sepulchre; have patience, look upon thy Son, and take leave

---

[2] O vere Dei nate, tu mihi pater, tu mihi filius, tu mihi sponsus, tu mihi anima eras! Nunc orbor patre, viduor sponso, desolor filio, uno perdito filio omnia perdo. De Lam. V. Mar.

[3] O quam libenter tunc posita fuissem viva cum filio meo, si fuisset voluntas ejus! Rev. 1. 1.

of him for the last time. "Then, oh my beloved Son," must the afflicted mother have said, "then shall I see thee no more? Receive then, this last time that I look upon thee, receive the last farewell from me thy dear mother, and receive my heart which I leave buried with thee." The Virgin, says St. Fulgentius, earnestly desired that her soul should be buried with the body of Christ.[4] And Mary herself made this revelation to St, Bridget: "I can truly say, that at the burial of my Son, one sepulchre contained as it were two hearts."[5]

Finally, they take the stone and close up in the holy sepulchre the body of Jesus, that great treasure, greater than any in heaven and on earth. And here let us remark, that Mary left her heart buried with Jesus, because Jesus was all her treasure: "Where your treasure is, there will your heart be also."[6] And where shall we keep our hearts buried? With creatures? In the mire? And why not with Jesus, who, although he has ascended to heaven, has wished to remain, not dead but alive, in the most holy Sacrament of the altar, precisely in order that he may have with him and possess our hearts? But let us return to Mary. Before quitting the sepulchre, according to St. Bonaventure, she blessed that sacred stone, saying: Oh happy stone, that doth now inclose that body which was contained nine months in my womb, I bless thee, and envy thee; I leave thee to guard my Son for me, who is my only good, my only love. And then turning to the eternal Father, she said: Oh Father, to thee I recommend him, who is thy Son and mine; and thus bidding a last farewell to her Son, and to the sepulchre, she returned to her own house. This poor mother went away so afflicted and sad, according to St. Bernard, that she moved many to tears even against their will: "Multos etiam invitos ad lacrymas provocabat;" so that wherever she passed, all wept who met her: "Omnes plorabant qui obviabant ei," and could not

---

[4] Animam cum corpore Christi contumulari Virgo vehementer exoptavit.
[5] Vere dicere possum quod sepulto filio meo quasi duo corda in uno sepulchro fuerunt. Rev. 1. 2, c. 21.
[6] Ubi thesaurus vester est, ibi et cor vestrum erit. Luc. xii. 34.

restrain their tears. And he adds that those holy disciples, and the women who accompanied her, mourned for her even more than for their Lord.[7]

St. Bonaventure says, that her two sisters covered her with a mourning cloak: The sisters of our Lady wrapped her in a veil as a widow, covering as it were her whole countenance.[8] And he also says that passing, on her return, before the cross, still wet with the blood of her Jesus, she was the first to adore it: Oh holy cross, she exclaimed, I kiss thee and adore thee; for thou art no longer an infamous wood, but a throne of love, and an altar of mercy, consecrated by the blood of the divine Lamb, who has been sacrificed upon thee, for the salvation of the world. She then leaves the cross and returns to her house; there the afflicted mother casts her eyes around, and no longer sees her Jesus; but instead of the presence of her dear Son, all the memorials of his holy life and cruel death are before her. There she is reminded of the embraces she gave her Son in the stable of Bethlehem, of the conversations held with him for so many years in the shop of Nazareth: she is reminded of their mutual affection, of his loving looks, of the words of eternal life that came forth from that divine mouth. And then comes before her the fatal scene of that very day; she sees those nails, those thorns, that lacerated flesh of her Son, those deep wounds, those uncovered bones, that open mouth, those closed eyes. Alas! what a night of sorrow was that night for Mary! The sorrowful mother turned to St. John, and said mournfully: Ah, John, where is thy master? Then she asked of Magdalen: Daughter, tell me where is thy beloved? Oh God! who has taken him from us? Mary weeps, and all those who are with her weep. And thou, oh my soul, dost thou not weep! Ah, turn to Mary, and say to her with St. Bonaventure: Let me, oh my Lady, let me weep; thou art innocent, I am guilty.[9] At least

---

[7] Super ipsam potius, quam super Dominum plangebant.
[8] Sorores Dominae velaverunt eam tamquam viduam; cooperientes quasi totum vultum.
[9] Sine, Domine mea, sine me flere; tu innocens es, ego sum reus.

entreat her to permit thee to weep with her: "Fac ut tecum lugeam." She weeps for love, and thou dost weep through sorrow for thy sins. And thus weeping, thou mayest have the happy lot of him of whom we read in the following example.

EXAMPLE

Father Engelgrave relates,[10] that a certain religious was so tormented by scruples, that sometimes he was almost driven to despair, but having great devotion to Mary, the mother of sorrows, he had recourse to her in the agony of his spirit, and was much comforted by contemplating her dolors. Death came, and the devil tormented him more than ever with scruples, and tempted him to despair. When, behold, our merciful mother, seeing her poor son so afflicted, appeared to him, and said to him: "And why, oh my son, art thou so overcome with sorrow, thou who hast so often consoled me by thy compassion for my sorrows?[11] Be comforted," she said to him; "Jesus sends me to thee to console thee; be comforted, rejoice, and come with me to paradise." And at these words the devout religious tranquilly expired, full of consolation and confidence.

PRAYER

My afflicted mother, I will not leave thee alone to weep; no, I wish to keep thee company with my tears. This grace I ask of thee today: obtain for me a continual remembrance of the passion of Jesus, and of thine also, and a tender devotion to them, that all the remaining days of my life may be spent in weeping for thy sorrows, oh my mother, and for those of my Redeemer. I hope that these dolors will give me the confidence and strength not to despair at the hour of my death, at the sight of the offences I have committed against

---

[10] Dom infra oct Nat. s. 2.
[11] Et tu, fili mi, cur moerore conficeris, qui in moerore meo toties me consolatus es?

my Lord. By these must I obtain pardon, perseverance, paradise, where I hope to rejoice with thee, and sing the infinite mercy of my God through all eternity: thus I hope, thus may it be. Amen, amen.

Whoever wishes to practise the devotion of reciting the chaplet of the dolors of Mary, will find it at the end of the book. I composed this many years since, and insert it anew here[12] for the convenience of the servants of Mary, whom I pray in their charity to recommend me to her when they meditate upon her dolors.

Oh Lady, who dost ravish the heart of men with thy sweetness, hast thou not ravished mine? Oh, ravisher of hearts, when wilt thou restore to me my heart? Do with it as with thine own, and place it in the side of thy Son. Then I shall possess what I hope for, because thou art our hope.[13]

---

[12] See the Section called, *The Little Rosary of the Seven Dolors of Mary*, p. 97.

[13] O Domina, quae rapis corda hominum dulcore, nonne cor meum rapuisti? O raptrix cordium, quando mihi restitues cor meum? Guberna illud cum tuo, et in latere filii colloca. Tune possidebo quod spero, quia tu es spes nostra. S. Bernard. Med. in Salv. Reg. ap. s. Bon. Stim. c. 19, part. 3.

HOW POWERFUL IS MARY IN PROTECTING THOSE WHO INVOKE HER IN TEMPTATIONS OF THE DEVIL

Not only is most holy Mary queen of heaven and of the saints, but also of hell and the devils, for she has bravely triumphed over them by her virtues. From the beginning of the world, God predicted to the infernal serpent the victory and the empire which our queen would obtain over him, when he announced to him that a woman would come into the world who should conquer him.[1] "I will put enmities between thee and the woman; she shall crush thy head."[2] And what woman was this enemy if not Mary, who, with her beautiful humility and holy life, always conquered him and destroyed his forces? St. Cyprian affirms that the mother of our Lord Jesus Christ was promised in that woman:[3] and hence he remarks that God did not use the words *I put*, but *I will put*, lest the prophecy should seem to appertain to Eve.[4] He said,

---

[1] From *The Glories of Mary*, Part One, Chapter IV, Section II
[2] Inimicitias ponam inter te et mulierem; ipsa conteret caput tuum. Gen. iii. 15.
[3] Mater Domini Jesn Christi in illa muliere promissa est.
[4] Non pono, sed ponam ne ad Evam pertinere videatur.

I will put enmity between thee and the woman, to signify that this his vanquisher was not the living Eve, but must be another woman descending from her, who was to bring to our first parents greater blessings, as St. Vincent Ferrer says, than those they had lost by their sin.[5]

Mary, then, is this great and strong woman who has conquered the devil, and has crushed his head by subduing his pride, as the Lord added: "She shall crush thy head."[6] Some of the commentators doubt whether these words refer to Mary or to Jesus Christ because, in the Septuagint version, we read: "He shall crush thy head."[7] But in our Vulgate, which is the only version approved by the Council of Trent, it is *She*, and not *He*. And thus St. Ambrose, St. Jerome, St. Augustine, St. John Chrysostom, and many others have understood it. However this may be, it is certain that the Son by means of the mother, or the mother by means of the Son, has vanquished Lucifer; so that this proud spirit, as St. Bernard tells us, has been ignominiously overpowered and crushed by this blessed Virgin.[8] Hence as a slave conquered in war, he is forced always to obey the commands of this queen. St. Bruno says that Eve, by yielding to the serpent, brought into the world death and darkness; but that the blessed Virgin, by conquering the devil, brought us life and light: and she has bound him so that he cannot move to do the least harm to her servants.[9]

Richard of St. Laurence gives a beautiful explanation to these words of Proverbs: "The heart of her husband trusteth in her, and he shall have no need of spoils."[10] Richard says: The heart of her husband, that is, Christ, trusts in her, and he shall have no need of spoils, for she will endow him with the

---

[5] Parentibus primis Virginem ab ipsis processuram; quae afferret majus bonum quam ipsi perdiderunt. Serm. 2, de Nat. Virg.

[6] Ipsa conteret caput tuum.

[7] Ipse conteret caput tuum.

[8] Sub Mariae pedibus conculcatus et contritus miseram patitur servitutem. Serm. in Sign. Magn.

[9] Et Eva mors, et caligo; in Maria, vita consistit, et lux. Illa a diabolo victa est; haec diabolum vicit et ligavit. Ap. Scala Franc. p. 4, c. 10.

[10] Confidit in ea cor viri sui, et spoliis non indigebit. Prov. xxxi. 11.

spoils which she has taken from the devil.[11] God has intrusted the heart of Jesus, as à Lapide expresses it, to the care of Mary, that she may procure for it the love of men; and thus he will not be in need of spoils, that is, of the conquest of souls, for she will enrich him with those souls of which she despoils hell, and which she has rescued from the demons by her powerful aid.

It is well known that the palm is the emblem of victory, and for this reason our queen has been placed on a high throne in the sight of all potentates, as a palm, the sign of certain victory, which all can promise themselves who have recourse to her. "I was exalted like a palm-tree in Cades."[12] That is, for a defence,[13] as blessed Albertus Magnus says: Oh, my children, Mary seems to say to us with these words, when the enemy assails you, lift your eyes to me, behold me and take courage; for in me, who defends you, you will behold, at the same time, your victory. So that recourse to Mary is the most certain means of overcoming all the assaults of hell; for she, as St. Bernardine of Sienna says, is queen over hell, and ruler of the spirits of evil, for she controls and conquers them.[14] And therefore Mary is called terrible against the power of hell, as an army set in array. "Terrible as an army set in array."[15] Set in array, because she knows how to array her powers, that is, her compassion and her prayers, to the confusion of the enemy and the benefit of her servants, who, in their temptations, invoke her powerful aid.

"As the vine I have brought forth a pleasant odor."[16] "I, like the vine," as the Holy Spirit puts it in her mouth to say, "have given fruit of sweet odor." "It is said," adds St. Bernard, on this passage, "that every venomous reptile shuns the

---

[11] Confidit in ea cor viri sui, scilicet Christi. Et spoliis non indigebit; ipsa enim quasi ditat sponsum suum, quibus spoliat diabolum.

[12] Quasi palma exaltata sum in Cades. Eccli. xxiv. 18

[13] Scilicet ad defendendum.

[14] Beata Virgo dominatur in regno inferni. Dicitur igitur domina daemonum, quasi domans daemones. Serm. 3, de Glor. Nom, Mar.

[15] Terribilis ut castrorum acies ordinata. Cant. vi, 3.

[16] Ego quasi vitis fructificavi suavitatem odoris. Eccli. xxiv. 23.

flowering vines."[17] As from vines all poisonous serpents flee, thus the demons flee from those fortunate souls in whom they perceive the odor of devotion to Mary. On this account she also is called a cedar: "I was exalted like a cedar in Libanus,"[18] not only because as the cedar is free from corruption so Mary is free from sin, but also because, as Cardinal Hugo remarks upon this passage, as the cedar with its perfume puts serpents to flight, so Mary with her sanctity puts to flight the devils.[19]

Victories were gained in Judea by means of the ark. Thus Moses conquered his enemies. "When the ark was lifted up, Moses said, Arise, oh Lord, and let thy enemies be scattered."[20] Thus Jericho was conquered; thus were the Philistines conquered; "for the ark of God was there."[21] It is well known that this ark was the type of Mary. As the ark contained the manna, thus Mary contained Jesus, whom the manna also prefigured, and by means of this ark, victories were gained over the enemies of earth and over hell.[22] Wherefore St. Bernardine of Sienna says that when Mary, the ark of the New Testament, was crowned queen of heaven, the power of hell over men was weakened and overthrown.[23]

"Oh, how the devils in hell," says St. Bonaventure, "tremble at Mary and her great name!"[24] The saint compares these enemies to those of whom Job makes mention and says: "He diggeth through houses in the dark...If the morning suddenly appear, it is to them the shadow of death."[25] Thieves enter houses in the dark to rob them, but when the dawn

---

[17] Aiunt de florescentibus vitibus omne reptile venantium excedere loco. Serm. 60, in Cant.

[18] Quasi cedrus exaltata sum in Libano. Eccli. xxiv. 17.

[19] Cedrus odore suo fugat serpentes, et beata Virgo daemones.

[20] Cum elevaretur arca, dicebat Moyses; Surge Domine, et dissipentur inimici tui. Num. x. 35.

[21] Erat enim ibi arca Dei. 1, Reg. xiv. 18.

[22] Arca continens manna, idest Christum, est B. Virgo, quae victoriam contra homines et daemones largitur. Cornel. a Lap.

[23] Quando elevata fuit Virgo gloriosa a celestia regna, daemonis potentia imminuta est et dissipata. Tom. 3, de B. V. Serm. 11.

[24] O quam tremenda est Maria daemonibus. Spec. Virg. c. 3.

[25] Perfodit in tenebris domos ... Si subito apparuerit aurora; arbitrantur umbram mortis. Job xxiv. 16, 17.

comes they flee, as if the image of death appeared to them. In the same manner, as St. Bonaventure expresses it, the demons enter into the soul in times of darkness, that is, when the soul is obscured by ignorance; they dig through the houses of our minds in the darkness of ignorance; but then, he adds, as soon as the grace and the mercy of Mary enter the soul, this beautiful aurora dissipates the darkness, and the infernal enemies flee as at the approach of death.[26] Oh, blessed is he who always, in his conflicts with hell, invokes the beautiful name of Mary!

In confirmation of this it was revealed to St. Bridget that God has given Mary such power over all evil spirits, that whenever they assail any of her servants who implore her aid, at the slightest sign from her they flee far away in terror, preferring that their pains should be redoubled rather than that Mary should domineer over them in this manner.[27]

À Lapide remarks upon the words with which the divine spouse praises his beloved bride, when he calls her the lily, and says that as the lily is among thorns, so is his beloved among the other daughters;[28] that, as the lily is a remedy against serpents and poisons, so the invocation of Mary is a special remedy for overcoming all temptations, particularly those of impurity, as they who have tried it have universally experienced.[29]

St. John of Damascus said, and every one may say the same who is so happy as to be devoted to this great queen: Oh, mother of God, if I trust in thee, I shall surely not be

---

[26] Perfodiunt in tenebris ignorantiae domos mentium nostrarum. Si subito supervenerit aurora, idest Mariae gratia, et misericordia, sic fugiunt, sicut omnes fugiunt mortem. In Spec. Virg.

[27] Super omnes etiam malignos spiritus ipsam sic potentem effecit, quod quotiescumque ipsi hominem Virginis auxilium implorantem impugnaverint, ad ipsius Virginis nutum illico pavidi procul diffugiunt; volentes potius suas poenas multiplicari, quam ejusdem Virginis potentiam super se taliter dominari. Serm, Ang. c. 20.

[28] Sicut lilium inter spinas, sic amica mea inter filias. Cant. ii. 2.

[29] Sicut lilium valet inter serpentes et venena, sic beatae Virginis invocatio singulare est remedium in omni tentatione, praesertim libidinis, ut experientia constat.

vanquished; for, defended by thee, I will pursue my enemies, and opposing to them thy protection and thy powerful support as a shield, I shall surely conquer them.[30] James the Monk, reputed a doctor among the Greek fathers, discoursing of Mary to our Lord, says: Thou, oh my Lord, hast given us this mother for a powerful defence against all our enemies.[31]

It is related in the Old Testament that the Lord guided his people from Egypt to the promised land, by day in a pillar of clouds, by night in a pillar of fire.[32] This pillar, now of clouds, now of fire, says Richard of St. Laurence, was a type of Mary and her double office, which she exercises continually in our behalf; as a cloud she protects us from the heat of divine justice, and as fire she protects us from demons.[33] Fire, as St. Bonaventure adds, for as wax melts at the approach of fire, thus the evil spirits lose all power in the presence of those souls who often call upon the name of Mary, and devoutly invoke her, and more than all, strive to imitate her.[34]

Oh, how the devils tremble, exclaims St. Bernard, if they only hear the name of Mary uttered![35] As men, says Thomas à Kempis, fall to the earth through fear, when a thunderbolt strikes near them, so fall prostrate the devils when but the name of Mary is heard.[36] How many noble victories have the servants of Mary not gained over these enemies by the power

---

[30] Insuperabilem spem tuam habens, O Deipara, servabor, Persequar inimicos meos, solam habens ut thoracem protectionem tuam, et omnipotens auxilium tuum. In Annunc. Dei Gen.

[31] Tu arma omni vi belli potentiora, trophaeumque invictum praestitisti.

[32] Per diem in columna nubis, et per noctem in columna ignis. Exod. xiii. 21.

[33] Ecce duo officia, ad quae data est nobis Maria, scilicet, ut nos protegat a calore solis justitiae, tamquam nubes, et tamquam ignis; ut omnes nos protegat contra diabolum. Lib. 7, de Laud. Virg.

[34] Fluunt sicut cera a facie ignis, ubi inveniunt crebram hujus nominis recordationem, devotam invocationem, solicitam imitationem. In Spec.

[35] In nomine Mariae omne genuflectitur, et daemones non solum pertimescunt, sed, audita hac voce, contremiscunt. Serm. sup. Miss.

[36] Expavescunt coeli reginam spiritus maligni et diffugiunt, audite somme eius, venit ab igne, tamquam tonitru de coelo factum sit, prosternuntur ad sanctae Mariae vocabulum. L. 4, ad Nov.

of her most holy name! Thus St Anthony of Padua conquered them, thus the blessed Henry Suso, thus many other lovers of Mary. It is related in the accounts of the missions to Japan that a great number of demons appeared in the form of ferocious animals to a certain Christian of that country, to alarm him and threaten him, but he spoke to them in these words: "I have no arms with which to terrify you; if the Most High permits it, do with me according to your pleasure. Meanwhile I use as my defence the most sweet names of Jesus and Mary." Hardly had he uttered these words, when behold, at the sound of those fearful names, the earth opened and those proud spirits were swallowed up. St. Anselm also asserts that he had seen and heard many persons who at the mention of the name of Mary were delivered from their dangers.[37]

"Very glorious, oh Mary, and wonderful," exclaims St. Bonaventure, "is thy great name. Those who art mindful to utter it at the hour of death, have nothing to fear from hell, for the devils at once abandon the soul when they hear the name of Mary."[38] And the saint adds that an earthly enemy does not so greatly fear a great army as the powers of hell fear the name and protection of Mary.[39] Thou, oh Lady, says St. Germanus, by the invocation alone of thy most powerful name, dost render thy servants secure from all the assaults of the enemy.[40] Oh, if Christians were mindful in temptations to invoke with confidence the name of Mary, it is certain that they would never fall; for, as blessed Alanus remarks, at the thunder of that great name, the devil flees and hell trembles.[41] This heavenly queen herself revealed to St. Bridget that even

---

[37] Saepe vidimus et andivimus plurimos homines, in suis periculis nominis recordari Mariae, et illico periculi malum evasisse. S. Ans. de Exc. Virg. c. 6.

[38] Gloriosum et admirabile est nomen tuum O Maria; qui illud retinent non expavescunt in puncto mortis; nam daemones audientes hoc nomen Mariae statim relinquunt animam. In Psalt. B. V.

[39] Non sic timent hostes visibiles castrorum multitudinem copiosam, sicut aereae potestates Mariae vocabulum, et patrocinium. Loc. cit.

[40] Tu servos tuos contra hostis invasiones, sola tui nominis invocatione tutos servas. Serm. de Zona. Virg.

[41] Satan fugit, infernus contremiscit, cum dico Ave Maria.

from the most abandoned sinners, who had wandered the farthest from God, and were most fully possessed by the devil, the enemy departs as soon as he hears her most powerful name invoked by them, if they do it with a true intention of amending.[42] But the Virgin added that if the soul does not amend, and with contrition quit its sins, the demons immediately return to it and hold it in their possession.[43]

EXAMPLE

In Reisberg there lived a Canon regular named Arnold, who was very devoted to the Blessed Virgin. Being at the point of death, he received the sacraments, and calling his religious to him, begged them not to leave him at the last moment. Scarcely had he said this, when he began to tremble violently and roll his eyes; cold sweat fell from him, and with an agitated voice he exclaimed: "Do you not see those demons who would seize me and carry me to hell?" Then he cried: "My brothers, invoke for me the help of Mary; I trust in her that she will give me the victory." They immediately began to recite the Litany of our Lady, and at the words, *Holy Mary, pray for him,* "Sancta Maria, ora pro eo," the dying man cried: "Repeat, repeat the name of Mary, for I am even now at the tribunal of God." He stopped for a moment, and then added: "It is true that I did it, but I have done penance for it." Then turning to the Virgin, he said: "Oh Mary, I shall be delivered if thou wilt help me." The demons soon after made another attack, but he defended himself by blessing himself with the crucifix, and invoking Mary. Thus he passed the whole night, but when morning dawned, Arnold, restored to serenity, joyfully said: "Mary, my Lady, and my refuge, has obtained for me pardon and salvation." Then, beholding the Virgin, who summoned him to follow her, he said: "I come, oh Lady, I come." He made an effort to rise, but not being able to follow

---

[42] Omnes daemones audientes hoc nomen, Maria, statim relinquunt animam quasi territi. L. 1, Rev. c. 9.

[43] Et revertuntur ad eam, nisi aliqua emendatio subsequatur. Lib. 1. Rev. c. 9.

her with the body, gently expiring, he followed her with his soul, as we hope, to the blessed kingdom of glory.[44]

PRAYER

Behold at thy feet, oh Mary my hope, a poor sinner who many times, through his own fault, has been the slave of hell. I know that I have often been conquered by the devil, because I have neglected to recur to thee, oh my refuge. If I had always sought thy protection, if I had invoked thee, I should never have fallen. I hope, oh my Lady, most worthy of love, that by thy help I have escaped the powers of hell, and that God has pardoned me. But I tremble for the future, lest I again fall into their power. I know that these enemies of mine have not lost all hope of reconquering me, and at this moment they are preparing new assaults and temptations. Oh, my queen and refuge, aid me. Shelter me beneath thy mantle, let me not become again their slave. I know that thou wilt succor me and give me victory whenever I invoke thee. I fear only that in my temptations I may forget thee, and neglect to call upon thee. This, then, is the grace, oh most holy Virgin, that I seek and wish from thee, that I may always remember thee, and especially when I find myself in conflict with the enemy; let me not then fail to invoke thee often with the words: "Oh Mary, help me; help me, oh Mary." And when, at length, the day of my last conflict with hell, the day of my death arrives, oh, my queen, powerfully assist me then, and remind me thyself to invoke thee more frequently, with the voice or with the heart, that expiring with thy most sweet name, and that of thy son Jesus on my lips, I may go to bless and praise thee, and never leave thy feet in paradise through all eternity. Amen.

---

[44] Father Auriemma, Affetti Scambiev. Tom. i. c, 7.

SELECTIONS FROM AN ENCYCLICAL OF POPE ST. PIUS X

AD DIEM ILLUM LAETISSIMUM

"On the Immaculate Conception"
By Pope St. Pius X
1904

The following selections present insights from the saintly Vicar of Christ, Pope St. Pius X, on the matter of Mary's role in the life and suffering of her Divine Son. His words, as the Supreme Teacher of the Church, are presented here for the benefit of the faithful, that they may read how, not only in the writings of the great Saints and Doctors of the Church like St. Alphonsus Liguori, but also from the very voice of the Church herself, do we receive these deep and rich teachings and reflections on the unique role entrusted to the Holy Mother of God.

On the Knowledge Mary Had of Jesus

"Through the Virgin, and through her more than through any other means, we have offered us a way of reaching the knowledge of Jesus Christ… [this] cannot be doubted when it is remembered that with her alone of all others Jesus was for thirty years united, as a son is usually united with a mother, in the closest ties of intimacy and domestic life. Who could better than His Mother have an open knowledge of the admirable mysteries of the birth and childhood of Christ, and above all of the mystery of the Incarnation, which is the beginning and the foundation of faith? Mary not only preserved and meditated on the events of Bethlehem and the facts which took place in Jerusalem in the Temple of the Lord, but sharing as she did the thoughts and the secret wishes of Christ, she may be said to have lived the very life of her Son." (7)

"Nobody ever knew Christ so profoundly as she did, and nobody can ever be more competent as a guide and teacher of the knowledge of Christ. Hence it follows, as We have already pointed out, that the Virgin is more powerful than all others as a means for uniting mankind with Christ. Hence too since, according to Christ Himself, *Now this is eternal life: That they may know thee the only truly God, and Jesus Christ whom thou hast sent,*[1] and since it is through Mary that we attain to the knowledge of Christ, through Mary also we most easily obtain that life of which Christ is the source and origin." (7-8)

---

[1] John xvii., 3

Mary's Role in Preparing Christ as the Victim for our Sins

"Moreover it was not only the prerogative of the Most Holy Mother to have furnished the material of His flesh to the Only Son of God, Who was to be born with human members,[2] of which material should be prepared the Victim for the salvation of men; but hers was also the office of tending and nourishing that Victim, and at the appointed time presenting Him for the sacrifice. Hence [there was] that uninterrupted community of life and labors of the Son and the Mother, so that of both might have been uttered the words of the Psalmist, *My life is consumed in sorrow and my years in groans.*[3] When the supreme hour of the Son came, beside the Cross of Jesus there stood Mary His Mother, not merely occupied in contemplating the cruel spectacle, but rejoicing that her Only Son was offered for the salvation of mankind, and so entirely participating in His Passion, that if it had been possible she would have gladly borne all the torments that her Son bore.[4] And from this community of will and suffering between Christ and Mary she merited to become most worthily the Reparatrix of the lost world[5] and Dispensatrix of all the gifts that Our Savior purchased for us by His Death and by His Blood." (12)

---

[2] S. Bede Ven. L. Iv. in Luc. xl.
[3] Ps xxx., 11
[4] S. Bonav. 1. Sent d. 48, ad Litt. dub. 4
[5] Eadmeri Mon. De Excellentia Virg. Mariae, c. 9

Mary's Role as Mediator between the Divine Head and the Mystical Body

"It cannot, of course, be denied that the dispensation of these treasures is the particular and peculiar right of Jesus Christ, for they are the exclusive fruit of His Death, who by His nature is the mediator between God and man. Nevertheless, by this companionship in sorrow and suffering already mentioned between the Mother and the Son, it has been allowed to the august Virgin to be the most powerful mediatrix and advocate of the whole world with her Divine Son.[6] The source, then, is Jesus Christ, *of whose fullness we have all received,*[7] *from whom the whole body, being compacted and fitly joined together by what every joint supplieth, according to the operation in the measure of every part, maketh increase of the body unto the edifying of itself in charity.*[8] But Mary, as St. Bernard justly remarks, is the channel[9]; or, if you will, the connecting portion, the function of which is to join the body to the head and to transmit to the body the influences and volitions of the head — We mean the neck. "Yes," says St. Bernardine of Sienna, "she is the neck of Our Head, by which He communicates to His mystical body all spiritual gifts."[10] (13)

---

[6] Pius IX. Ineffabilis
[7] John i., 16
[8] Ephesians iv., 16
[9] Serm. de temp on the Nativ. B. V. De Aquaeductu n. 4
[10] Quadrag. de Evangel. aetern. Serm. x., a. 3, c. iii.

The Highest Degree of Mary's Virtues Shone at the Foot of the Cross

"Now if it becomes children not to omit the imitation of any of the virtues of this most Blessed Mother, we yet wish that the faithful apply themselves by preference to the principal virtues which are, as it were, the nerves and joints of the Christian life — we mean faith, hope, and charity towards God and our neighbor. Of these virtues the life of Mary bears in all its phases the brilliant character; but they attained their highest degree of splendor at the time when she stood by her dying Son. Jesus is nailed to the cross, and the malediction is hurled against Him that "He made Himself the Son of God."[11] But she unceasingly recognized and adored the divinity in Him. She bore His dead body to the tomb, but never for a moment doubted that He would rise again. Then the love of God with which she burned made her a partaker in the sufferings of Christ and the associate in His passion; with him moreover, as if forgetful of her own sorrow, she prayed for the pardon of the executioners although they in their hate cried out: "His blood be upon us and upon our children."[12] (21)

---

[11] John xix., 7
[12] Matth. xxvii., 25

SACRAMENTALS IN HONOR OF OUR LADY OF SORROWS

THE BLACK SCAPULAR & THE ROSARY OF THE SEVEN DOLORS

by
Charles D. Fraune

St. Alphonsus Liguori, in his masterpiece, *The Glories of Mary*, told a story about a specific Sacramental that is related to Our Lady of Sorrows. This Sacramental is known as the *Black Scapular*. Before explaining the history of that Scapular, and before looking at the blessing that is placed upon it by the Church, let us listen again[1] to his account of the power and the spiritual effects it can bring to those who use it devoutly.

> A young man in Perugia once promised the devil that if he would help him to commit a sinful act which he desired to do, he would give him his soul; and he gave him a writing to that effect, signed with his blood. The evil deed was committed, and the devil demanded the

---

[1] See "On the Fifth Dolor of Mary," p. 62 in this book.

performance of the promise. He led the young man to a well, and threatened to take him body and soul to hell if he would not cast himself into it. The wretched youth, thinking that it would be impossible for him to escape from his enemy, climbed the well-side in order to cast himself into it, but terrified at the thought of death, he said to the devil that he had not the courage to throw himself in, and that, if he wished to see him dead, he himself should thrust him in. The young man wore about his neck *the scapular of the sorrowing Mary*; and the devil said to him: "Take off that scapular, and I will thrust you in." But the youth, seeing the protection which the divine mother still gave him through that scapular, refused to take it off, and after a great deal of altercation, the devil departed in confusion. The sinner repented, and grateful to his sorrowful mother, went to thank her, and presented a picture of this case, as an offering, at her altar in the new church of Santa Maria, in Perugia.[2]

The origin of the black scapular of the Sorrowful Mother, or *of the Seven Dolors of the Blessed Virgin Mary*, dates back to 1240, to the seven men who founded the Order of the Servants of Mary, also called the *Servites*. As they were preparing to found this Order, they had a vision of Our Lady presenting them with black garments with which they were to be clad in their new Order, in memory of the sufferings of her sorrowful heart. After experiencing the vision, they then founded this new religious Order. Thus, the black scapular originated with this vision and it appears to be the first scapular to be adopted and worn by the laity.[3]

---

[2] *The Glories of Mary*, 1888, p.575-6. Emphasis mine
[3] Miller, Raymond J., C.Ss.R. *The Five Scapulars: Facts About the Five Scapulars*. Brooklyn, NY: Redemptorist Fathers, 1961, 6.

The black scapular is an official Sacramental of the Church, formerly reserved to this same Order of Servites. By that, it is to be understood that this Sacramental was under the spiritual care of the Order of Servites and administered exclusively by them as a result of their Order being the one through which Our Lady brought this gift to the whole Church. In recent times, all *reserved* Sacramentals were put under the care of every priest, allowing more universal access to all of the Sacramentals.

To properly understand the graces that the Church intends for the faithful to receive from this Sacramental, we must look at the official ritual the Church has prescribed her priests to use when blessing this sacred garment. This is to be found in the second volume of the *Rituale Romanum.*[4]

Before blessing the scapular, the Church blesses the one who is about to receive it. She prays, "Let this candidate be delivered from all vexations of the world and of the flesh, let him (her) be safeguarded against the snares of the devil, through the intercession of the Blessed Virgin Mary, of St. Augustine and St. Philip and our holy fathers, the seven founders of our Order, may he (she) come to the inheritance of true joy."

Turning her attention to the scapular itself, the Church prays, "Bless this garment, which our holy fathers have sanctioned to be worn by us in token of innocence and lowliness, and in memory of the Seven Sorrows of the Blessed Virgin Mary. So let this servant (handmaid) who wears it be invested in soul and body with thee, our Savior."

The priest then bestows the blessed garment on the individual, saying, "Receive, beloved brother (sister), the habit of the Blessed Virgin Mary, the special badge of her servants, as a reminder of the Seven Sorrows which she endured during the life and death of her Sole-Begotten Son. And having been invested with it, mayest thou, through her intercession, live forever and ever."

---

[4] *Rituale Romanum*, Volume II, originally published in 1950, Caritas Publishing, 2017, 269. The English title is the "Roman Ritual."

While this ends the blessing and investiture with the black scapular, the ritual also includes the giving of the Rosary of the Seven Sorrows. The ritual advises the one who just received the scapular, "Receive the rosary of the Blessed Virgin Mary, designed to commemorate her Seven Sorrows, so that whilst thy lips utter her praises, thy heart may fully commiserate with her in her sufferings."

The Church also has a blessing for this Rosary of the Seven Sorrows, also called *the Rosary of the Seven Dolors*.[5] As the reader can clearly see, this Rosary, like the scapular, is endowed with the grace to drive away the evil one. This would resemble the impact of the black scapular as depicted in the story recounted by St. Alphonsus Liguori. Here is the blessing for the Rosary:

> "Wherefore, we humbly beg Thee of Thine immeasurable goodness to bless and sanctify this rosary, which Thy faithful Church has consecrated to the memory of the Seven Sorrows of the Mother of Thy Son. And let it be endowed with such power of the Holy Spirit, that, whosoever recites it or carries it on his person or treasures it with reverence in his home, may at all times and in all places be delivered from every foe, visible and invisible, during this life, and at the hour of death attain the grace of being presented to Thee by the Blessed Virgin Mary, crowned with the aureole of good works."

The full ritual blessing for both the Scapular and the Rosary are provided at the end of this book. This blessing, as a reminder, is only to be done by priests. The *Rituale Romanum* blessings were not permitted to be performed by deacons. Further, it is best to perform the blessing in Latin since only some of these blessings have been authorized by

---

[5] *Rituale Romanum*, Volume II, 274.

the Church to be done in the vernacular (English) language. The priest could then recite the blessing in English for the edification of the faithful who are present.

These two devotions, revealed by Our Lady and adopted and approved by the Church as official Sacramentals, highlight the importance of having a devotion to Our Lady of Sorrows. As St. Alphonsus told us above:

> In order to understand how much the Virgin is pleased by our remembrance of her dolors, it is sufficient to relate, that in the year 1239, she appeared to seven of her servants, who then became the founders of the order of the Servants of Mary, with a black garment in her hand, and told them that if they wished to please her, they should often meditate upon her dolors; and therefore she wished, in memory of them, that they would hereafter wear that garment of mourning.[6]

By taking upon ourselves this "garment of mourning," in union with these seven holy men, and at the prompting of Holy Mother Church, we also obey this call from Our Lady and likewise share in the spiritual and temporal benefits that flow from her powerful intercession.

---

[6] See page 26.

THE LITTLE ROSARY OF THE SEVEN DOLORS OF MARY

from
The Glories of Mary

V. O God, come to my assistance.[1]
R. *O Lord, make haste to help me.*

O my mother, enable my heart to share thy sorrow for the
death of thy Son.

First Dolor

I pity thee, O my afflicted mother, on account of the first
sword of sorrow that pierced thee, when in the temple, by the
prophecy of St. Simeon, all the cruel sufferings that men
would inflict on thy beloved Jesus were represented to thee,
which thou hadst already learned from the holy Scriptures,
even to his death before thy eyes upon the infamous wood of
the cross, exhausted of blood and abandoned by all, and thou

---

[1] The original wording was *Incline unto mine aid, oh God, &c.*, here changed to the
modern English usage. - SDP

without the power to defend or relieve him. By that bitter memory, then, which for so many years afflicted thy heart, I pray thee, O my queen, to obtain for me the grace that always in life and in death I may keep impressed upon my heart the passion of Jesus and thy sorrows.

Our Father, Hail Mary, Glory be to the Father.[2]

O my mother, enable my heart to share thy sorrow for the death of thy Son.

Second Dolor

I pity thee, O my afflicted mother, on account of the second sword that pierced thee when thou didst behold thy innocent Son, so soon after his birth, threatened with death by those very men for whom he had come into the world, so that thou wast obliged to flee with him by night secretly into Egypt. By the many hardships, then, that thou, a delicate young virgin, in company with thy exiled infant, didst endure in the long and wearisome journey through rough and desert countries, and in thy sojourn in Egypt, where, being unknown and a stranger, thou didst live all those years poor and despised, I pray thee, O my beloved Lady, to obtain for me the grace to suffer with patience, in thy company till death, the trials of this miserable life, that I may be able in the next to be preserved from the eternal sufferings of hell deserved by me.

Our Father, Hail Mary, Glory be to the Father.

O my mother, enable my heart to share thy sorrow for the death of thy Son.

---

[2] Other translations of *The Glories of Mary* suggest *seven* Hail Marys with this Little Rosary. – SDP

Third Dolor

I pity thee, O my afflicted mother, on account of the third sword that pierced thy heart at the loss of thy dear son, Jesus, who remained absent from thee in Jerusalem for three days, when not seeing thy beloved one by thy side, and not knowing the cause of his absence, I conceive, my loving Queen, how in these nights thou didst not repose, and didst naught but sigh for him who was thy only good. By the sighs, then, of those three days, for thee so long and bitter, I pray thee to obtain for me the grace never to lose my God, that I may always live closely united to God, and thus united with him, depart from this world.

Our Father, Hail Mary, Glory be to the Father.

O my mother, enable my heart to share thy sorrow for the death of thy Son.

Fourth Dolor

I pity thee, O my afflicted mother, on account of the fourth sword that pierced thy heart, in seeing thy Jesus condemned to death, bound with ropes and chains, covered with blood and wounds, crowned with thorns, and falling under the weight of the heavy cross which he bore on his bleeding back when going like an innocent lamb to die for love of us. Thine eye then met his eye, and your glances were so many cruel arrows with which each wounded the loving heart of the other. By this great grief, then, I pray thee to obtain for me the grace to live wholly resigned to the will of my God, joyfully bearing my cross with Jesus to the last moment of my life.

Our Father, Hail Mary, Glory be to the Father.

O my mother, enable my heart to share thy sorrow for the death of thy Son.

Fifth Dolor

I pity thee, O my afflicted mother, on account of the fifth sword that pierced thy heart, when on Mount Calvary thou didst behold thy beloved son, Jesus, dying slowly before thy eyes, amid so many insults, and in anguish, on that hard bed of the cross, without being able to give him even the least of those comforts which the greatest criminals receive at the hour of death. And I pray thee by the anguish which thou, O my most loving mother, didst suffer together with thy dying Son, and by the tenderness thou didst feel when, for the last time he spoke to thee from the cross, and taking leave of thee, left all of us to thee in the person of St. John, as thy children; and thou, still constant, didst behold him bow his head and expire; I pray thee to obtain for me the grace, by thy crucified love, to live and die crucified to everything in this world, in order to live only to God through my whole life, and thus to enter one day paradise, to enjoy him face to face.

Our Father, Hail Mary, Glory be to the Father.

O my mother, enable my heart to share thy sorrow for the death of thy Son.

Sixth Dolor

I pity thee, O my afflicted mother, on account of the sixth sword which pierced thy heart, when thou didst see the kind heart of thy Son pierced through and through after his death – a death endured for those ungrateful men, who, even after his death, were not satisfied with the tortures they had inflicted upon him. By this cruel sorrow, then, which was

104

wholly thine, I pray thee to obtain for me the grace to abide in the heart of Jesus, who was wounded and opened for me; in that heart, I say, which is the beautiful abode of love, where all the souls who love God repose; and that living there, I will never love or think of anything but God. Most holy Virgin, thou canst do it; from thee I hope for it.

Our Father, Hail Mary, Glory be to the Father.

O my mother, enable my heart to share thy sorrow for the death of thy Son.

Seventh Dolor

I pity thee, O my afflicted mother, on account of the seventh sword that pierced thy heart, on seeing in thy arms thy Son who had just expired, no longer fair and beautiful as thou didst once receive him in the stable of Bethlehem, but covered with blood, livid, and lacerated by wounds which exposed his very bones. My Son, thou saidst, my Son, to what has love brought thee? And when he was borne to the sepulchre, thou didst wish to accompany him thyself, and help to put him in the tomb with thy own hands; and, bidding him a last farewell, thou hast left thy loving heart buried with thy Son. By all the anguish of thy pure soul, obtain for me, O mother of fair love, pardon for the offences that I have committed against my God, whom I love, and of which I repent with my whole heart. Wilt thou defend me in temptations? Assist me at the hour of my death, that, being saved by the merits of Jesus and thine, I may come one day with thy aid, after this miserable exile, to sing in paradise the praises of Jesus and thine through all eternity. Amen.

Our Father, Hail Mary, Glory be to the Father.

O my mother, enable my heart to share thy sorrow for the death of thy Son.

Pray for us, O most sorrowful Virgin,
That we may be made worthy of the promises of Christ.

Let us pray

O God, at whose passion, according to the prophecy of Simeon, the sword of sorrow pierced through the most sweet soul of the glorious Virgin and Mother, Mary, grant that we, who commemorate and reverence her dolors, may experience the blessed effect of Thy passion, who livest and reignest world without end. Amen.

BENEDICT XIII. granted two hundred days indulgence for every "Our Father" and every "Hail Mary" to those who recite this little crown in the churches of the Servites of Mary, and has granted the same favor to those who recite it in any place whatever on Fridays or any day during Lent; and on other days, one hundred days for every "Our Father" and "Hail Mary." To those who recite it entire, seven years. To those who recite it for a year, plenary indulgence, applicable to the souls in purgatory. Moreover, let it be observed that there are seven hundred years of indulgence for the dead granted by Clement XII to those who say, kneeling, the De Profundis *at the ringing of the bell.*[3]

---

[3] This refers to the practice of praying for the dead at the final ringing of the bell in the evening, done either one hour after the last Angelus bell, or at nine o'clock in the evening. Clement XII enriched this practice with an indulgence in an effort to extend this practice beyond just the city of Rome. - SDP

SOME DEVOUT PRAYERS OF VARIOUS SAINTS TO THE HOLY MOTHER OF GOD

The following prayers are included in this volume,[1] not only for the use of the faithful, but also because they show the great idea which the saints entertained of the power and mercy of Mary, and their great confidence in her patronage.

---

[1] i.e. *The Glories of Mary*

Prayer of St. Ephrem

Oh, immaculate and wholly pure Virgin Mary! Mother of God, Queen of the universe, our most excellent Lady, thou art superior to all the saints, thou art the only hope of the Fathers, and the joy of the blessed. By thee we have been reconciled to our God. Thou art the only advocate of sinners, the secure haven of the shipwrecked. Thou art the consolation of the world, the redemption of captives, the joy of the sick, the comfort of the afflicted, the refuge and salvation of the whole world. Oh, great princess! Mother of God! Cover us with the wings of thy compassion: have pity on us. We have no hope but in thee, oh most pure Virgin! We are given to thee and consecrated to thy service; we bear the name of thy servants; do not permit Lucifer to draw us down to hell. Oh, immaculate Virgin! we are under thy protection; therefore, unitedly we have recourse to thee, and supplicate thee to prevent thy Son, whom our sins have offended, from abandoning us to the power of the devil.

Oh, full of grace! illuminate my intellect, loosen my tongue that it may sing thy praises, and especially the Angelic Salutation, so worthy of thee. I salute thee, oh peace! oh joy! oh salvation and consolation of the whole world! I salute thee, oh greatest of miracles! paradise of delight! secure haven of those who are in danger! fountain of grace! mediatrix of God and men!

PRAYER OF ST. BERNARD

We raise our eyes to thee, oh Queen of the world. After having committed so many sins we must appear before our Judge, and who will appease him? None can do it better than thou, oh blessed Lady, who hast loved him so much, and hast been so tenderly beloved by him. Open thy heart, then, oh mother of mercy, to our sighs and prayers. We fly to thy protection; appease the anger of thy Son and restore us to his favor. Thou dost not abhor the sinner, however loathsome he may be; thou dost not despise him, if he sends up his sighs to thee, and with contrition asks thy intercession; thou, with thy kind hand, dost deliver him from despair; thou dost encourage him to hope, dost comfort him, and dost not leave him until thou hast reconciled him to his Judge.

Thou art that only one in whom the Saviour found his rest, and with whom he has deposited all his treasures. Hence all the world, oh Mary, honors thy chaste womb, as the temple of God, where the salvation of the world had its beginning. In thee was effected the reconciliation between God and man. Thou art the enclosed garden, oh great Mother of God, whose flowers have never been gathered by the sinner's hand. Thou art the beautiful garden, in which God has placed all the flowers which adorn the Church, such as the violet of thy humility, the lily of thy purity, and the rose of thy charity. Who can be compared to thee, oh mother of grace and of beauty? Thou art the paradise of God. From thee hath sprung up the fountain of living water, that waters all the earth. Oh, how many favors hast thou bestowed upon the world, by meriting to be the channel of the waters of salvation!

Of thee the Holy Ghost speaks when he says: Who is she that arises like the dawn, fair as the moon, bright as the sun? Thou art, then, come into the world, oh Mary, as a resplendent dawn, preceding, with the light of thy sanctity, the coming of the Sun of Justice. The day in which thou didst appear in the world may truly be called the day of salvation, the day of grace. Thou art fair as the moon; for as there is no planet more like the sun, so there is no creature more like God than thou art. The moon illuminates the night with the light which it receives from the sun, and thou dost illuminate our darkness, with the splendor of thy virtues; and thou art fairer than the moon, because in thee is found neither stain nor shade. Thou art bright as the sun, I mean as that Sun which hath created the sun; he has been chosen among all men, and thou among all women. Oh sweet, oh great, oh most lovely Mary, thy name cannot be pronounced by anyone that thou dost inflame with thy love; neither can those who love thee think of thee without feeling themselves encouraged to love thee more.

Oh, blessed Lady, help our weakness. And who is more fit to speak to our Lord Jesus Christ than thou, who dost enjoy, so near to him, his sweet conversation? Speak, speak, oh Lady, because thy Son listens, and thou wilt obtain from him whatever thou shalt demand.

PRAYER OF ST. GERMANUS

Oh, my only Lady, who art the sole consolation which I receive from God; thou who art the only celestial dew that doth soothe my pains; thou who art the light of my soul when it is surrounded with darkness; thou who art my guide in my journeyings, my strength in my weakness, my treasure in my poverty; balm for my wounds, my consolation in sorrow; thou who art my refuge in misery, the hope of my salvation, graciously hear my prayer, have pity on me, as is befitting the mother of a God who hath so much love for men. Thou who art our defence and joy, grant me what I ask; make me worthy of enjoying with thee that great happiness which thou dost enjoy in heaven. Yes, my Lady, my refuge, my life, my help, my defence, my strength, my joy, my hope, make me to come with thee to paradise. I know that, being the mother of God, thou canst obtain this for me if thou wilt. Oh Mary, thou art omnipotent to save sinners, thou needest nothing else to recommend us to thee, for thou art the mother of true life.

PRAYER OF THE ABBOT OF CELLES, SURNAMED THE IDIOT

Draw me after thee, oh Virgin Mary, that I may run to the odor of thy perfumes. Draw me, for I am held back by the weight of my sins and by the malice of my enemies. As no one goes to thy Son unless the divine Father draws him, so I would dare to say, in a certain sense, that no one goes to him if thou dost not draw him with thy holy prayers. It is thou who teachest true wisdom; thou who dost obtain pardon for sinners, because thou art their advocate. It is thou who dost promise glory to him who honors thee, because thou art the treasurer of graces.

Thou hast found grace with God, oh most sweet Virgin, because thou hast been preserved from the stain of original sin, filled with the Holy Spirit, and hast conceived the Son of God. Thou hast received all these graces, oh Mary most humble, not only for thyself, but also for us, that thou mayest help us in all our necessities. And thou, indeed, dost so; thou dost succor the good by preserving them in grace; and the bad, by bringing them to receive the divine mercy; thou dost aid the dying by protecting them against the snares of the devil; and thou dost aid them also after death by receiving their souls and leading them to the kingdom of the blessed.

PRAYER OF ST. METHODIUS

Thy name, oh Mother of God, is full of all graces and divine blessings. Thou hast comprehended him who is incomprehensible, and nourished him who nourishes all living creatures. He who fills heaven and earth and is Lord of all, has chosen to have need of thee, since thou hast clothed him with that garment of flesh that he had not before. Rejoice, oh Mother and handmaid of God! Rejoice! Rejoice! Thou hast for a debtor him to whom all creatures owe their being. We are all debtors to God, but God is a debtor to thee. Hence it is, oh most holy Mother of God, that thou hast greater goodness and greater charity than all the other saints, and more than all others hast near access in heaven to God, because thou art his mother. Ah, we pray thee that we may celebrate thy glories, and may know how great is thy goodness, being mindful of us and of our miseries.

PRAYER OF ST. JOHN DAMASCENE

I salute thee, oh Mary! Thou art the hope of Christians; receive the petition of a servant who tenderly loves thee, especially honors thee, and places in thee all the hope of his salvation. From thee I have life, thou dost restore me to the favor of thy Son; thou art the certain pledge of my salvation. I implore thee, then, to deliver me from the burden of my sins; dispel the darkness of my mind; banish earthly affections from my heart; repel the temptations of my enemies, and so order my life, that I may reach, by thy means and by thy guidance, the eternal felicity of paradise.

PRAYER OF ST. ILDEPHONSUS

I come to thee, oh mother of God, I supplicate thee to obtain for me the pardon of my sins, and that I may be purified from all the errors of my life. I pray thee to grant me thy grace, that I may unite myself with affection to thy Son and to thee; to thy Son as to my God, to thee as to the mother of my God.

PRAYER OF ST. ATHANASIUS

Hearken, oh most holy Virgin, to our prayers, and remember us. Dispense to us the gifts of thy riches, and the abundant graces with which thou art filled. The archangel salutes thee and calls thee *full of grace*. All nations call thee *blessed*; the whole hierarchy of heaven blesses thee, and we, who are of the terrestrial hierarchy, also say to thee: "Hail, full of grace, the Lord is with thee." Pray for us, oh Mother of God, our Lady and our Queen.

PRAYER OF ST. ANDREW OF CANDIA, or OF JERUSALEM

I salute thee, oh full of grace! the Lord is with thee. I salute thee, oh cause of our joy, by whom the sentence of our condemnation has been already revoked, and changed into a judgment of benediction. I salute thee, oh temple of the glory of God, sacred house of the King of Heaven. Thou art the reconciliation of God with men. I salute thee, oh mother of our joy. In truth, thou art blessed, for thou alone, among all women, hast been found worthy of being the mother of thy Creator. All nations call thee blessed.

Oh Mary, if I put my confidence in thee, I shall be saved; if I am under thy protection, I have nothing to fear, for to be thy servant is to have the secure armor of salvation, which God does not grant except to those whom he will save.

Oh, mother of mercy, appease thy Son. Whilst thou wast on earth thou didst only occupy a small part of it; but now that thou art raised above the highest heaven, the whole world considers thee as the propitiatory of all nations. We supplicate thee, then, oh holy Virgin, to grant us the aid of thy prayers with God; prayers which are dearer and more precious to us than all the treasures of earth; prayers that render God inclined to forgive our sins; and wilt thou obtain for us abundant graces to receive the pardon of them and to practise virtue? prayers that conquer our enemies, confound their designs, and triumph over their forces.

PRAYER OF ST. ANSELM

We pray thee, oh most blessed Lady, by that grace which God bestowed on thee when he so greatly exalted thee, rendering all things possible to thee with him; we pray thee to obtain for us that the fulness of grace which thou hast merited may make us to share thy glory. Be pleased, oh most merciful Lady, to procure for us the good for which God consented to become man in thy chaste womb. Be not slow to hear us. If thou wilt deign to supplicate thy Son, he at once will graciously hear thee. It is enough that thou wilt save us, for then we cannot but be saved. Who can restrain the bowels of thy compassion? If thou hast not compassion on us, thou who art the mother of mercy, what will become of us when thy Son shall come to judge us?

Come, then, to our succor, oh most compassionate mother, without regarding the multitude of our sins. Remember again and again that our Creator has taken human flesh from thee, not to condemn sinners, but to save them. If thou hadst been made Mother of God only for thine own advantage, it might be said that it would be to thee of little importance whether we were saved or condemned; but God has clothed himself with thy flesh for thy salvation and for that of all men. What will it avail us that thou art so powerful and so glorious, if thou dost not render us partakers of thy felicity? Aid us and protect us; remember the need we have of thy assistance. We recommend ourselves to thee; save us from damnation, and make us serve and love eternally thy Son, Jesus Christ.

PRAYER OF ST. PETER DAMIAN

Holy Virgin, Mother of God, succor those who implore thy assistance. Turn to us. But, having been deified, as it were, hast thou forgotten men?[2] Ah, certainly not. Thou knowest in what peril thou hast left us, and the wretched condition of thy servants; no, it is not befitting a mercy so great to forget so great misery as ours. Turn to us with thy power, because he who is powerful hath given thee omnipotence in heaven and on earth. To thee nothing is impossible, for thou canst raise even the despairing to the hope of salvation. Thou must be compassionate as thou art powerful.

Turn to us, also, in thy love. I know, oh my Lady, that thou art all kindness, and dost love us with a love that no other love can surpass. How dost thou appease the anger of our Judge when he is on the point of punishing us for our offences! All the treasures of the mercy of God are in thy hands. Ah, may it never happen that thou shouldst cease from doing us good: thou seekest the occasion of saving all sinners, and of bestowing thy mercy upon them; for thy glory increases when, by thy means, penitents are pardoned, and the pardoned come to paradise. Turn, then to us, that we may come to see thee in heaven; for the greatest glory we can obtain, next to seeing God, is to see thee, to love thee, and to be under thy protection. Ah, graciously hear us, since thy Son wishes to honor thee, by granting all thy requests.

---

[2] This term refers to our glorification in Heaven, the culmination of having been made "partakers of the divine nature" (2 Peter 1:4) through Baptism. – SDP

PRAYER OF ST. WILLIAM, BISHOP OF PARIS

Oh, Mother of God, I fly to thee and I implore thee not to cast me off, for the whole Church of the faithful calls thee, and proclaims thee the Mother of Mercy. Thou art so dear to God that thou art always graciously heard; thy compassion has never been wanting to anyone; thy most gracious condescension has never despised any sinner, however enormous his sin, who has recommended himself to thee. Does the Church falsely and in vain call thee her advocate, and the refuge of the unhappy? No; let my sins never prevent thee from exercising thy great office of mercy by which thou art the advocate, the mediatrix of reconciliation, the only hope, and the most secure refuge of sinners. Let it never be that the mother who, for the good of the whole world, brought forth him who is the fountain of mercy, should refuse her mercy to any sinner who has recourse to her. It is thy office to reconcile God to man; let then thy compassion move thee to help me, for it is greater than all my sins.

PRAYER TO THE MOST HOLY MARY
TO BE SAID EVERY DAY
AT THE END OF THE VISIT

Oh, most holy, immaculate Virgin, and my mother Mary, to thee who art the mother of my Lord, the queen of the world, the advocate, the hope, the refuge of sinners, I, the most miserable of all, have recourse today. I adore thee, oh great queen, and thank thee for all the favors thou hast hitherto granted me, especially for having delivered me from hell, which I have so often deserved. I love thee, oh most amiable Lady, and through the love I bear thee promise that I will always serve thee, and do all that I can that thou mayest also be loved by others. I place in thee all my hopes of salvation; accept me for thy servant, and receive me under thy mantle, oh thou mother of mercy. And since thou art so powerful with God, deliver me from all temptations, or obtain for me the strength to conquer them always until death. From thee I ask a true love for Jesus; from thee I hope to die a good death. Oh, my mother, by the love thou bearest to God, I pray thee always to help me, but most of all at the last moment of my life. Do not leave me until thou seest me actually safe in heaven, blessing thee, and singing thy mercies throughout all eternity. Amen. Thus I hope. Thus may it be.

The Blessing of the Black Scapular of Our Lady of Sorrows

&

The Blessing of the Rosary of Our Lady of Sorrows

from
the Rituale Romanum

8

Benedictio et Impositio Scapularis Nigri
Septem Dolorum B. Mariae Virg.

(Propria Ordinis Servorum B. M. V.)

Suscepturus Habitum genuflectit; et Sacerdos, superpelliceo ac stola alba indutus, dicit:

℣. Adjutórium nostrum in nómine Dómini.

℟. Qui fecit caelum et terram.

℣. Dóminus vobíscum.   ℟. Et cum spíritu tuo.

Pro uno vel una	Pro pluribus
Orémus. Oratio	**Orémus.** Oratio

OMNIPOTENS sempitérne Deus, qui morte Unigéniti tui mundum collápsum restauráre dignátus es, ut nos a morte aetérna liberáres, et ad gáudia regni caeléstis perdúceres: réspice, quaésumus, super hanc famíliam servórum tuórum, in nómine beatíssimae Vírginis Septem Dolóribus sáuciae congregátam, de cujus grémio hic fámulus tuus (haec fámula tua) esse cupit; ut augeátur númerus tibi fidéliter serviéntium, et ómnibus saéculi et carnis perturbatiónibus liberátus (-a) et a láqueis diáboli secúrus (-a) intercessióne ejúsdem beátae

OMNIPOTENS sempitérne Deus, qui morte Unigéniti tui mundum collápsum restauráre dignátus es, ut nos a morte aetérna liberáres, et ad gáudia regni caeléstis perdúceres: réspice, quaésumus, super hanc famíliam servórum tuórum, in nómine beatíssimae Vírginis Septem Dolóribus sáuciae congregátam, de cujus grémio hi fámuli tui (hae fámulae tuae) esse cúpiunt; ut augeátur númerus tibi fidéliter serviéntium, et ómnibus saéculi et carnis perturbatiónibus liberáti (-ae) et a láqueis diáboli secúri (-ae) intercessióne ejúsdem beátae Ma-

8

Blessing and Investiture With Black Scapular of Our Lady of Sorrows

(Reserved to the Order of Servites)

The candidate for the scapular is kneeling. The priest, vested in surplice and white stole, says:

℣. Our help is in the name of the Lord.
℟. Who made heaven and earth.
℣. The Lord be with you.   ℟. And with thy spirit.

For one	For several
Let us pray. *Prayer*	Let us pray. *Prayer*

ALMIGHTY and everlasting God! Thou didst deign to lift up a fallen world by the death of thy Sole-Begotten Son, in order to deliver us from eternal condemnation, and to lead us to the joys of the heavenly kingdom. Look down, we beseech thee, on this family of thy clients, congregated in the name of the Blessed Virgin of the Seven Sorrows, in whose bosom this servant (handmaid) of thine seeks refuge. Thus may the number of them who faithfully serve thee be increased. And let this candidate be delivered from all vexations of the world and of the flesh, let him (her) be safeguarded against the snares of the devil, and through the intercession of the

ALMIGHTY and everlasting God! Thou didst deign to lift up a fallen world by the death of thy Sole-Begotten Son, in order to deliver us from eternal condemnation, and to lead us to the joys of the heavenly kingdom. Look down, we beseech thee, on this family of thy clients, congregated in the name of the Blessed Virgin of the Seven Sorrows, in whose bosom these servants (handmaids) of thine seek refuge. Thus may the number of them who faithfully serve thee be increased. And let these candidates be delivered from all vexations of the world and of the flesh, let them be safeguarded against the snares of the devil, and through the intercession of

Maríae Vírginis, beatórum Augustíni et Philíppi ac septem nostrórum beatórum Patrum Ordinis Fundatórum, vera gáudia possídeat. Per eúmdem Christum Dóminum nostrum. ℟. Amen.

ríae Vírginis, beatórum Augustíni et Philíppi ac septem nostrórum beatórum Patrum Ordinis Fundatórum, vera gáudia possídeant. Per eúmdem Christum Dóminum nostrum. ℟. Amen.

Conversus ad Habitum super Altare positum, Sacerdos dicit:

Pro uno vel una

Orémus.   Oratio

DÓMINE Jesu Christe, qui tégumen nostrae mortalitátis indúere dignátus es, obsecrámus imménsam largitátis tuae abundántiam: ut hoc genus vestimentórum, quod sancti Patris nostri, ad innocéntiae humilitatísque indícium, in memóriam Septem Dolórum beátae Vírginis Maríae nos ferre sanxérunt, ita bene ✠ dícere dignéris; ut, qui (quae) illis fúerit indútus (indúta), córpore páriter et ánimo índuat te Salvatórem nostrum: Qui vivis et regnas in saécula saeculórum. ℟. Amen.

Pro pluribus

Orémus.   Oratio

DÓMINE Jesu Christe, qui tégumen nostrae mortalitátis indúere dignátus es, obsecrámus imménsam largitátis tuae abundántiam: ut hoc genus vestimentórum, quod sancti Patris nostri, ad innocéntiae humilitatísque indícium, in memóriam Septem Dolórum beátae Vírginis Maríae nos ferre sanxérunt, ita bene ✠ dícere dignéris; ut, qui (quae) illis fúerint indúti (-ae), córpore páriter et ánimo índuant te Salvatórem nostrum: Qui vivis et regnas in saécula saeculórum. ℟. Amen.

Aspergit Habitum aqua benedicta, dicens:

Aspérges me, Dómine, hyssópo et mundábor: lavábis me, et super nivem dealbábor.

Deinde benedicit coronam Septem Dolorum B. Mariae Virg., dicens:
Orémus. Omnípotens et miséricors Deus, etc., ut infra, pag. 274, et coronam aspergit aqua benedicta.

Blessed Virgin Mary, of St. Augustine and St. Philip and our holy fathers, the seven founders of our Order, may he (she) come to the inheritance of true joy. Through the selfsame Christ our Lord. ℞. Amen.

the Blessed Virgin Mary, of St. Augustine and St. Philip and our holy fathers, the seven founders of our Order, may they come to the inheritance of true joy. Through the selfsame Christ our Lord. ℞. Amen.

Turning toward the habit which is placed on the altar, the priest says:

For one

Let us pray.　　Prayer

O LORD Jesus Christ, Who didst condescend to clothe thyself with our wounded nature, we humbly beg thee of thine immeasurable goodness to bless ✠ this garment, which our holy fathers have sanctioned to be worn by us in token of innocence and lowliness, and in memory of the Seven Sorrows of the Blessed Virgin Mary. So let this servant (handmaid) who wears it be invested in soul and body with thee, our Savior. Thou Who livest and reignest for endless ages. ℞. Amen.

For several

Let us pray.　　Prayer

O LORD Jesus Christ, Who didst condescend to clothe thyself with our wounded nature, we humbly beg thee of thine immeasurable goodness to bless ✠ this garment, which our holy fathers have sanctioned to be worn by us in token of innocence and lowliness, and in memory of the Seven Sorrows of the Blessed Virgin Mary. So let these servants (handmaids) who wear it be invested in soul and body with thee, our Savior. Thou Who livest and reignest for endless ages. ℞. Amen.

He sprinkles the scapular with holy water, saying:

Sprinkle me with hyssop, O Lord, and I shall be clean: wash me and I shall be whiter than snow.

Then he blesses the rosary of the Seven Dolors, using the prayer **Almighty and merciful God** *given below (p. 275), and sprinkling the rosary with holy water.*

Mox Sacerdos imponit Habitum cuilibet coram se genuflexo, dicens:

Pro uno vel una	Pro pluribus
Accipe, caríssime frater (caríssima soror), hábitum beátae Maríae Vírginis, singuláre signum servórum suórum, in memóriam Septem Dolórum, quos ipsa in vita et morte Unigéniti Fílii sui sustínuit; ut ita indútus (-a), sub ejus patrocínio, perpétuo vivas. ℟. Amen.	Accípite, caríssimi fratres (caríssimae soróres), hábitum beátae Maríae Vírginis, singuláre signum servórum suórum, in memóriam Septem Dolórum, quos ipsa in vita et morte Unigéniti Fílii sui sustínuit; ut ita indúti (-ae), sub ejus patrocínio, perpétuo vivátis. ℟. Amen.

Postea coronam porrigit, dicens:

Accipe corónam beátae Maríae Vírginis in memóriam Septem Dolórum suórum contéxtam, ut, dum eam ore laudáveris, ejus poenas toto corde compatiáris. ℟. Amen.	Accípite corónam beátae Maríae Vírginis in memóriam Septem Dolórum suórum contéxtam, ut, dum eam ore laudavéritis, ejus poenas toto corde compatiámini. ℟. Amen.

Deinde personam (personas) benedicit, dicens:

Benedíctio Dei omnipoténtis, Patris, et Fílii, ✠ et Spíritus Sancti, descéndat super te (vos), et máneat semper. ℟. Amen.

9

Benedictio Coronae Septem Dolorum B. Mariae Virg.

(Propria ejusdem Ordinis)

Sacerdos, superpelliceo ac stola alba indutus, dicit:

℣. Adjutórium nostrum in nómine Dómini.
℟. Qui fecit caelum et terram.

The priest invests the candidate (who is kneeling) with the scapular, saying the words:

For one	For several
Receive, beloved brother (sister), the habit of the Blessed Virgin Mary, the special badge of her servants, as a reminder of the Seven Sorrows which she endured during the life and death of her Sole-Begotten Son. And having been invested with it, mayest thou, through her intercession, live forever and ever. R/. Amen.	Receive, beloved brothers (sisters), the habit of the Blessed Virgin Mary, the special badge of her servants, as a reminder of the Seven Sorrows which she endured during the life and death of her Sole-Begotten Son. And having been invested with it, may you, through her intercession, live forever and ever. R/. Amen.

Then he hands the rosary to the person, saying:

Receive the rosary of the Blessed Virgin Mary, designed to commemorate her Seven Sorrows, so that whilst thy lips utter her praises, thy heart may fully commiserate with her in her sufferings. R/. Amen.	Receive the rosary of the Blessed Virgin Mary, designed to commemorate her Seven Sorrows, so that whilst your lips utter her praises, your heart may fully commiserate with her in her sufferings. R/. Amen.

Lastly he blesses the person(s) with the words:

May the blessing of almighty God, Father, Son, ✝ and Holy Spirit come upon thee (you) and remain for all time. R/. Amen.

9

Blessing of the Rosary of the Seven Dolors

(Reserved to the Order of Servites)

The priest, vested in surplice and white stole, says:

V/. Our help is in the name of the Lord.
R/. Who made heaven and earth.

℣. Dóminus vobíscum.

℟. Et cum spíritu tuo.

Orémus.   Oratio

OMNÍPOTENS et miséricors Deus, qui propter nímiam caritá-
tem, qua dilexísti nos, Fílium tuum unigénitum, Dóminum
nostrum Jesum Christum, pro redemptióne nostra de caelis ad
terram descéndere, carnem suscípere, et crucis torméntum subíre
voluísti: obsecrámus imménsam cleméntiam tuam; ut hanc
corónam, in memóriam septem dolórum Genitrícis Fílii tui ab
Ecclésia tua fidéli dicátam, bene ☩ dícas, et sanctí ☩ fices, et ei
tantam Spíritus ☩ Sancti virtútem infúndas, ut, quicúmque eam
recitáverit, ac secum portáverit, atque in domo sua reverénter
tenúerit, ab omni hoste visíbili et invisíbili, semper et ubíque in
hoc saéculo liberétur, et in éxitu suo a beatíssima Vírgine María
tibi, bonis opéribus coronátus, praesentári mereátur. Per eúmdem
Christum Dóminum nostrum. ℟. Amen.

Deinde Sacerdos aspergit coronam aqua benedicta.

10

Formula Brevior Benedicendi Coronam
Septem Dolorum B. Mariae Virg.

(Propria ejusdem Ordinis)

(Approbata a S. R. C. die 11 Febr. 1925)

Haec formula tantummodo privatim adhiberi potest, si quando,
ratione circumstantiarum, valde incommodum sit longiorem adhibere.

AD LAUDEM et glóriam Deíparae Vírginis Maríae, in memóriam Dolórum quos ipsa in vita et morte ejúsdem Fílii sui
Dómini nostri Jesu Christi sustínuit, bene ☩ dicátur et sancti ☩
ficétur haec coróna: in nómine Patris, et Fílii, ☩ et Spíritus
Sancti. ℟. Amen.

℣. The Lord be with you.

℟. And with thy spirit.

Let us pray. Prayer

ALMIGHTY and merciful God! On account of thy boundless love for us, thou hast willed that thy Sole-Begotten Son, our Lord Jesus Christ, should come upon earth for our salvation, should assume flesh and undergo the torment of the Cross. Wherefore, we humbly beg thee of thine immeasurable goodness to bless ✠ and sanctify ✠ this rosary, which thy faithful Church has consecrated to the memory of the Seven Sorrows of the Mother of thy Son. And let it be endowed with such power of the Holy ✠ Spirit, that, whosoever recites it or carries it on his person or treasures it with reverence in his home, may at all times and in all places be delivered from every foe, visible and invisible, during this life, and at the hour of death attain the grace of being presented to thee by the Blessed Virgin Mary, crowned with the aureole of good works. Through the selfsame Christ our Lord. ℟. Amen.

The priest sprinkles the rosary with holy water.

10

Short Form for Blessing the Rosary of the Seven Dolors

(Reserved to the Order of Servites)

(Approved by the Congregation of Sacred Rites on Feb. 11, 1925)

This form may be employed only in a private manner, whenever through force of circumstances it would be very inconvenient to use the longer form.

MAY this rosary be blessed ✠ and sanctified, ✠ to the praise and glory of the Virgin Mary, Mother of God, and in remembrance of the sorrows which she endured during the life and death of her Son, our Lord Jesus Christ. In the name of the Father, and of the Son, ✠ and of the Holy Spirit. ℟. Amen.

Slaying Dragons Press Classics

Slaying Dragons Press Classics is a new endeavor though one which has long been a desire of the Slaying Dragons Apostolate. In particular, there has been a desire to bring into print the marvelous and largely forgotten works of the master of morality and the spiritual life, St. Alphonsus Liguori.

With the desire to bring back into print many of his excellent writings, there has also been a felt need to make these writings intelligible to the modern Christian mind, often under-catechized and very much immersed in a materialistic and secular culture. Many Christians, even among the devout, have been deprived of the traditional teachings of the Church in the modern era. Great Christian writers such as St. Alphonsus Liguori are, therefore, greatly needed by the modern Church.

Slaying Dragons Press Classics intends to bring back many of his writings, presenting them in a way that preserves the integrity of the original and also presents some helpful analysis to assist the reader in remembering the key teachings.

This effort of bring back into print lost and marvelous writings of St. Alphonsus Liguori will not, God willing, be limited to this great Doctor of the Church alone. It is the hope that this effort will be able to present many more lost spiritual treasures to the faithful of today.

Slaying Dragons Press

Slaying Dragons Press, founded in 2021, is the fruit of a spiritual work begun in 2016 which sought to find new ways to bring people the joy and beauty of the Catholic Faith. By God's Providence, what began under the name *The Retreat Box* has grown into *The Slaying Dragons Apostolate* and *Slaying Dragons Press.*

This work is a grassroots apostolate which thrives on support and endorsements from those who enjoy these books. As a result, fans of the books and supporters of the mission help increase the reach of *Slaying Dragons Press* by telling friends, family, priests, religious, and Bishops about these books.

Please consider supporting this work in any way that you can. While *Slaying Dragons Press* is *not* a non-profit, financial support is always welcome. Please visit SlayingDragonsPress.com for ways to support this apostolate. If you do not have a copy of the other celebrated books we have published, get one today!

Support this work on **Patreon**
~patreon.com/**theslayingdragonsapostolate**

Subscribe to our website for discounts and news
~SlayingDragonsPress.com/pages/**Subscribe**

Popular Titles
from
Slaying Dragons Press Classics

The Life of St. Alphonsus Liguori, by a Member of the Order of Mercy (1886)

A Christian's Rule of Life *(with Darts of Fire)*, by St. Alphonsus Liguori

Sanctifying Pregnancy*: In the Light of the Joyful Mysteries of the Rosary*, by Margaret Place (1954)

Novena to the Holy Spirit*: Prayers and Meditations in Preparation for Pentecost*, by St. Alphonsus Liguori

The Scourge of Demons: *A Classic Manual (1576) on Exorcism and Spiritual Warfare*, by Fr. Girolamo Menghi, OFM

Popular Titles
from
Slaying Dragons Press

Slaying Dragons: *What Exorcists See & What We Should Know*

The Rise of the Occult: *What Exorcists & Former Occultists Want You to Know*

The Occult Among Us: *Exorcists and Former Occultists Expose the Nature of This Modern Evil*

Slaying Dragons - Prepare for Battle: *Applying the Wisdom of Exorcists to Your Spiritual Warfare*
   -   (a study guide, manual, and companion book to Slaying Dragons)

Swords and Shadows: *Navigating Youth Amidst the Wiles of Satan*

Come Away By Yourselves: *A Guide to Prayer for Busy Catholics*

Slaying Dragons is also available in Swedish, Spanish, and Portuguese.

Slaying Dragons Press